The
GOSPEL
of JESUS

*according to
the Jesus Seminar*

ROBERT W. FUNK
and the JESUS SEMINAR

First Edition

Library of Congress Cataloguing-in-Publication data available
ISBN 0-944344-74-7

The GOSPEL *of* JESUS

TABLE OF CONTENTS

Introduction

THE GOSPEL OF JESUS is a composite gospel created out of the short stories told about and words ascribed to Jesus in the ancient gospels. The selection of anecdotes and sayings was dictated by the decisions of the Fellows of the Jesus Seminar and reported in *The Five Gospels* and *The Acts of Jesus*. The arrangement of the words and reports was based, in part, on the Gospel of Mark. In other respects, the clustering of reports was suggested by the forms of stories, and the grouping of sayings and parables reflects common or related topics. In constructing a gospel in this fashion, we have done no more than imitate the practices of the first evangelists.

The authors of the ancient gospels and of other genres of literature freely plundered the work of their predecessors in composing their own texts. Plagiarism was an unknown concept and copyright had yet to be conceived. Moreover, authors did not always give their predecessors credit for the passages they borrowed. New compositions were written out by hand and often presented as solely the product of the new authors.

The composers of the New Testament gospels created their gospels in the same way. The author of the Gospel of Mark—the earliest of the four New Testament gospels—wrote down stories he had learned from oral storytellers and arranged these in a sequence suggested by topic and form, for the most part; he did not know the actual order of events. In addition, Mark may have had a few brief written texts, such as a compendium of parables or a collection of miracle stories, from which he copied.

Matthew and Luke then made use of Mark as the narrative basis for the gospels they created, but they freely rearranged and edited Mark. Into Mark they inserted

1

material from a collection of sayings, the Sayings Gospel Q, which did not survive as an independent text; it survives only to the extent it was incorporated into Matthew and Luke. Matthew and Luke varied considerably in the way they made use of their sources, Mark and Q.

We do not know the history of the Fourth Gospel. Some scholars have concluded that the Gospel of John drew on an early source, perhaps a gospel of "signs" or a compendium of miracle stories. The author may also have made use of synoptic traditions known to him from Mark, Matthew, and Luke. He did not hesitate to modify his sources while expanding them greatly by incorporating other oral traditions and by adding a healthy dose of his own creative imagination.

It is possible, in the judgment of many specialists, that collections of Jesus' parables and sayings were put in writing as early as 50–60 C.E. The Sayings Gospel Q may have been one such written collection. The origin of the Gospel of Thomas may also go back to this early period. Neither of these gospels is known in its original form. Three Greek fragments dating to the second century indicate that a Greek version of Thomas differed from the Coptic version discovered at Nag Hammadi.

Scholars have been unable to determine with certitude when the first gospels were reduced to writing. They speculate that Mark was composed in the decade of the 70s; Matthew and Luke were probably written a decade or two later. The Fourth Gospel probably appeared at the end of the first century. However, no physical remains of any of these early editions have survived the ravages of time. The earliest papyrus fragments date to the middle of the second century, and these are but tiny scraps containing only a few words. The first substantial pieces of any of the gospels that have survived from antiquity are dated to the end of the second century, almost 175 years after the death of Jesus and at least 100 years after their first editions.

In the Roman world, the preservation of individual documents depended on the activity of professional scribes who made copies by hand. Scribes often made mistakes in the copies they produced, with the consequence that no two copies of the same text were identical. There was a tendency, moreover, for scribes to edit the texts they copied. Scholars believe the gospels, like other documents, went through more than one "edition." The Gospel of Thomas, for example, went through several editions, as suggested above.

It is likely that the canonical gospels were also known in more than one form. The Gospel of John was almost certainly revised and augmented at least twice in its early history, as its multiple endings suggest. In earlier editions, Matthew and Luke probably began not with the birth and childhood narratives but with the preaching of John the Baptist, just as in the case of Q and Mark. The birth narratives were probably supplementary prefaces to those gospels added at a second stage.

Because of the close link between reports of appearances of the risen Jesus and the authority of those to whom he was alleged to have appeared, the canonical gospels went their separate ways in developing appearance stories. The diversity in these stories tacked onto the end of the gospels owes to the fact that Mark, the principal source of Matthew and Luke, did not contain any appearance stories.

The gospels rapidly became public documents. The publication of such documents meant that some patron or sponsor was willing to assume the costs connected with scribal reproduction. Often only one copy of a document would be made, unless demand grew for additional copies. If the sponsor were sufficiently wealthy, multiple copies might be commissioned. In the fourth century, the Emperor Constantine is known to have authorized Eusebius of Caesarea to commission the production of fifty copies of the entire Bible. So far as we know, none of those copies has survived, if in fact they were actually made. But the production of multiple copies of a single document would have been a rare phenomenon in the ancient world.

In constructing *The Gospel of Jesus* we have done no more than follow the precedents set by authors and editors of ancient gospels and other kinds of records. We have borrowed the contents of this new gospel from ancient texts, adding only a few transitional phrases, such as "Jesus said" or "Jesus used to tell his disciples" in introducing sayings or parables, and even these are exact replicas of phrases found in the original texts.

We have arranged the material by topic and kind of story, with the exception of a few major events. We assume that Jesus was born before he died and that prior to his public career he was a follower of John the Baptist. The minimal chronology that appears in this new gospel has been borrowed from the Gospel of Mark. Since even those traces of sequence were probably fictive, the order of events and clusters of sayings are the result of editorial decisions and do not necessarily reflect historical chronology.

The headings in the new gospel are also the work of the editor. Heads have the effect of suggesting what particular sayings meant or how certain stories were understood. It is impossible to avoid such suggestive overtones. Readers should be aware that alternative clustering and sequences are entirely possible. Indeed, the segments collected in the new gospel might serve as a do-it-yourself kit for those who wish to compose their own gospels.

Three other attempts to create new gospels have appeared. Stephen Mitchell created *The Gospel According to Jesus*, which is his own selection and translation of stories taken from the ancient gospels.[1]

Reynolds Price has also produced new translations of the Gospels of Mark and John, and then has gone on to create his own gospel, telling stories selected from ancient gospels in his own words. His translations tend to be paraphrases rather than close approximations of the underlying Greek text.[2]

James P. Carse has created an entirely fictional gospel he calls *The Gospel of the Beloved Disciple*. He has let his vivid imagination invent parables and events in the style of Jesus. The result is a delightful story that both entertains and instructs.[3]

The Gospel of Jesus is an indirect product of the Seminar. The materials selected were dictated by the two reports of the Seminar, *The Five Gospels* (1993) and *The Acts of Jesus* (1998). The editor has included all the red and pink sayings and reports (items that are probably historical), along with a smattering of reports that fell into the gray category (items that are possibly historical), and even a few words and phrases that were colored black (probably fictive).

The gray items chosen were those that came close to a pink weighted average but fell short, usually as the result of the presence of some fictive or misleading element. For example, on the cluster Children in the Marketplace (9:1–5), some Fellows voted gray or black because Jesus refers to himself as "the son of Adam," which was taken by those Fellows as a messianic title placed on the lips of Jesus by Christian believers. However, the phrase can also be understood as a way of referring to oneself as an ordinary human being in the third person. To justify inclusion, the editor has here translated the phrase as "this mother's son," precisely to avoid the Christian title.

In addition, the editor has occasionally included narrative elements colored black by the Fellows. In general,

1. *The Gospel According to Jesus: A New Translation and Guide to His Essential Teachings for Believers and Unbelievers* (New York: HarperCollins Publishers, 1991). 2. *Three Gospels* (New York: Scribners, 1996). 3. *The Gospel of the Beloved Disciple* (Harper SanFrancisco, 1997).

these are transitional phrases supplied by the evangelists out of their imaginations to give the story some narrative coherence. To cite one further instance: in the account of the death of John the Baptist (Mark 6:14–29), the editor has included vv. 25–26 in modified form (GJes 6:10–11), which, although colored black, is needed to understand the role of Herodias in the death of John. In this, as in other cases, nothing has been included that misrepresents or contradicts the character of Jesus mirrored in the red and pink material.

Another way of expressing the restrictions imposed on the editor is to say that nothing has been included that is not believed to be historical or can be said to be a "true fiction" (fictive but true to the character of Jesus and others as represented by the authentic material). An extended example of an anecdote colored gray but believed to be a "true fiction" is the story of the woman accused of adultery (6:21–30). While the Seminar regarded this fragment from an unknown gospel as invented, they thought it true to the disposition of the historical Jesus.

The editor has also modified stories in those cases where the Fellows decided reports were a combination of fiction and fact by leaving out gray and black elements. However, the editor has not augmented the text with his own fictions. In this respect, the editorial procedure has been to include only reports found in one or the other of the ancient sources. Unlike the ancient gospel authors, he did not create new events out of his own imagination nor did he provide individual reports with a new comprehensive narrative frame.

The translation used is the Scholars Version, a version created by the Fellows of the Jesus Seminar and employed in the reports of the Seminar and published separately as *The Complete Gospels*.

The
GOSPEL
of JESUS

Birth, childhood & family of Jesus

JESUS WAS A DESCENDANT of Abraham. ²Jesus' parents were named Joseph and Mary. ³Jesus was born when Herod was king. ⁴Eight days later, when the time came to circumcise him, they gave him the name Jesus. ⁵Many in Jesus' hometown asked, "This is the carpenter, isn't it? ⁶Isn't he Mary's son? ⁷And who are his brothers, if not James and Judas and Simon? And who are his sisters, if not our neighbors?" ⁸Phillip tells Nathanael, "We have found Jesus, Joseph's son, from Nazareth. ⁹"From Nazareth?" Nathanael said to him. "Can anything good come from that place?" ¹⁰Then he goes home, and once again a crowd gathers, so they could not even grab a bite to eat. ¹¹When his relatives heard about it, they came to get him. (You see, they thought he was out of his mind.) ¹²Jesus' family was resentful of him. ¹³On his visit to Jerusalem, Paul says, "I saw no other apostle except James the Lord's brother." ¹⁴James and Cephas and John were acknowledged pillars of the church in Jerusalem. ¹⁵The risen Jesus appeared to James.

1   *John the Baptist & Jesus*

A voice in the wilderness

John the Baptizer appeared in the wilderness calling for baptism and a change of heart that lead to forgiveness of sins. [2]And everyone from the Judean countryside and all the residents of Jerusalem streamed out to him and got baptized by him in the Jordan River, admitting their sins. [3]And John wore a mantle made of camel hair and had a leather belt around his waist and lived on locusts and raw honey.

[4]John would call out: "Change your ways because Heaven's imperial rule is closing in."

[5]John would say to the crowds that came out to get baptized by him, "You slimy bastards! Who warned you to flee from the impending doom? [6]Well then, start producing fruits suitable for a change of heart, and don't even start saying to yourselves, 'We have Abraham for our father.' Let me tell you, God can raise up children for Abraham right out of these rocks. [7]Even now the axe is aimed at the root of the trees. So every tree not producing choice fruit gets cut down and tossed into the fire."

[8]The crowds would ask him, "So what should we do?"

[9]And he would tell them, "Whoever has two shirts should share with someone who has none; whoever has food should do the same."

[10]Toll collectors also came to get baptized, and they would ask him, "Teacher, what should we do?"

[11]He told them, "Charge nothing above the official rates."

[12]Soldiers also asked him, "And what about us?"

[13]And he said to them, "No more shakedowns! No more frame-ups either! And be satisfied with your pay."

1:15–16
MARK 1:7–8
Matt 3:11; Luke 3:16
Source: Mark
Cf. John 1:15, 26–27

1:17
MARK 1:9
Matt 3:13; Luke 3:21
Source: Mark

1:18–20
LUKE 3:18–20
Mark 1:14; Matt 4:12
Sources: Mark, Q

1:21–31
MATT 4:1–11
Luke 4:1–13
Source: Q

¹⁴The people were filled with expectation and everyone was trying to figure out whether John might be the Anointed.

¹⁵John's answer was the same to everyone: "Someone more powerful than I will succeed me, whose sandal straps I am not fit to bend down and untie. ¹⁶I have been baptizing you with water, but he will baptize you with holy spirit."

Jesus is baptized

¹⁷During that same period Jesus came from Nazareth, Galilee, and was baptized in the Jordan by John.

John is imprisoned

¹⁸And so, with many other exhortations John preached to the people. ¹⁹But Herod the tetrarch, who had been denounced by John over the matter of Herodias, ²⁰topped off all his other crimes by shutting John up in prison.

Jesus is tested

²¹Then Jesus was guided into the wilderness by the spirit to be put to the test by the devil. ²²And after he had fasted 'forty days and forty nights,' he was famished.

²³And the tester confronted him and said, "To prove you're God's son, order these stones to turn into bread."

²⁴He responded, "It is written, 'Human beings are not to live on bread alone, but on every word that comes out of God's mouth.'"

²⁵Then the devil conducts him to the holy city, sets him on the pinnacle of the temple, ²⁶and says to him, "To prove you're God's son, jump off; remember, it is written, 'To his heavenly messengers he will give orders about you,' and 'with their hands they will catch you, so you won't even stub your toe on a stone.'"

²⁷Jesus said to him, "Elsewhere it is written, 'You are not to put the Lord your God to the test.'"

²⁸Again the devil takes him to a very high mountain and shows him all the empires of the world and their splendor, ²⁹and says to him, "I'll give you all these, if you will kneel down and pay homage to me."

³⁰Finally Jesus says to him, "Get out of here, Satan! Remember, it is written, 'You are to pay homage to the Lord your God, and you are to revere him alone.'"

³¹Then the devil leaves him, and heavenly messengers arrive out of nowhere and look after him.

2   *Jesus announces the good news*

A voice in Galilee

After John was locked up, Jesus came to Galilee proclaiming God's good news. ²His message went:

Citizens of the kingdom

Congratulations
³Congratulations, you poor!
God's domain belongs to you.
⁴Congratulations, you hungry!
You will have a feast.
⁵Congratulations, you who weep now!
You will laugh.

Children in God's domain

⁶And they would bring children to him so he could lay hands on them, but the disciples scolded them. ⁷Then Jesus grew indignant when he saw this and said to them: "Let the children come up to me, don't try to stop them. After all, God's domain belongs to people like that. ⁸I

swear to you, whoever doesn't accept God's imperial rule the way a child would, certainly won't ever set foot in God's domain!"

Kingdom banquet

⁹Jesus used to tell this parable:

Someone was giving a big dinner and invited many guests. ¹⁰At the dinner hour the host sent his slave to tell the guests: "Come, it's ready now." ¹¹But one by one they all began to make excuses. The first said to him, "I just bought a farm, and I have to go and inspect it; please excuse me." ¹²And another said, "I just bought five pairs of oxen, and I'm on my way to check them out; please excuse me." ¹³And another said, "I just got married, and so I cannot attend." ¹⁴So the slave came back and reported these excuses to his master. ¹⁵Then the master of the house got angry and instructed his slave: "Quick! Go out into the streets and alleys of the town, and usher in the poor, the crippled, the blind, and the lame."

¹⁶And the slave said, "Sir, your orders have been carried out, and there's still room."

¹⁷And the master said to the slave, "Then go out into the roads and the country lanes, and force people to come in so my house will be filled. ¹⁸Believe you me, not one of those who were given invitations will taste my dinner."

Good news

Mustard seed

¹⁹The disciples said to Jesus, "Tell us what Heaven's imperial rule is like."

He said to them, "It's like a mustard seed. ²⁰It's the smallest of all seeds, but when it falls on prepared soil, it produces a large plant, which becomes a shelter for birds of the sky."

18   *Gospel of Jesus*

Leaven

²¹When speaking of the kingdom, Jesus would say: "What does God's imperial rule remind me of? ²²It is like leaven that a woman took and concealed in fifty pounds of flour until it was all leavened."

Empty jar

²³Jesus used to say, "The Father's imperial rule is like a woman who was carrying a jar full of meal. ²⁴While she was walking along a distant road, the handle of the jar broke and the meal spilled behind her along the road. ²⁵She didn't know it; she hadn't noticed a problem. ²⁶When she reached her house, she put the jar down and discovered that it was empty."

Ask, seek, knock

²⁷"Ask—it'll be given to you; seek—you'll find; knock—it'll be opened for you. ²⁸Rest assured: everyone who asks receives; everyone who seeks finds; and for the one who knocks it is opened."

On anxieties

²⁹He used to say to his disciples, "That's why I tell you: Don't fret about life—what you're going to eat—or about your body—what you're going to wear. ³⁰Remember, there is more to living than food and clothing. ³¹Think about the crows: they don't plant or harvest, they don't have storerooms or barns. Yet God feeds them. You're worth a lot more than the birds! ³²Can any of you add an hour to life by fretting about it? ³³So if you can't do a little thing like that, why worry about the rest? ³⁴Think about how the wild lilies grow: they don't slave and they never spin. Yet let me tell you, even Solomon at the height of his glory was never decked out like one of them. ³⁵If God dresses up the grass in the field, which is here today and tomorrow is tossed into an oven, it is

2:36–37
MATT 6:9, 11
cf. LUKE 11:3
Source: Q

2:38–39
LUKE 12:6–7
Matt 10:29–31
Source: Q

3:1–5
MARK 1:16–20
Matt 4:18–22
Source: Mark

3:6–7
MARK 2:14
Matt 9:9; Luke 5:27–28
Source: Mark

surely more likely that God cares for you, you who don't take anything for granted!"

Request for bread
³⁶"Our Father,
³⁷ "Give us the bread we need for the day."

God and sparrows
³⁸Jesus said, "What do sparrows cost? A dime a dozen? Yet not one of them is overlooked by God. ³⁹In fact, even the hairs of your head have all been counted. Don't be so timid: You're worth more than a flock of sparrows."

3   *Disciples & discipleship*

First disciples

Simon Peter and Andrew, James and John
As he was walking along by the Sea of Galilee, he spotted Simon and Andrew, Simon's brother, casting their nets into the sea—since they were fishermen—²and Jesus said to them: "Become my followers and I'll have you fishing for people!"

³Right then and there they abandoned their nets and followed him.

⁴When he had gone a little farther, he caught sight of James, Zebedee's son, and his brother John mending their nets in the boat. ⁵Right then and there he called out to them as well, and they left their father Zebedee behind in the boat with the hired hands and accompanied him.

Levi
⁶As Jesus was walking along, he caught sight of Levi, the son of Alphaeus, sitting at the toll booth, and he says to him, "Follow me!"

⁷And Levi got up and followed him.

Women companions of Jesus

⁸Jesus traveled through towns and villages, preaching and announcing the good news of God's imperial rule. ⁹His male disciples were with him, and also some women whom he had cured of evil spirits and diseases: Mary, the one from Magdala, from whom seven demons had taken their leave, ¹⁰and Joanna, the wife of Chuza, Herod's steward, and Susanna, and many others, who provided for them out of their resources.

Discipleship

Foxes have dens

¹¹As they were going along the road, someone said to him, "I'll follow you wherever you go."

¹²And Jesus said to him, "Foxes have dens, and birds of the sky have nests; but this mother's child has nowhere to rest his head."

Let the dead bury the dead

¹³To another he said, "Follow me."

But he said, "First, let me go and bury my father."

¹⁴Jesus said to him, "Leave it to the dead to bury their own dead; but you, go out and announce God's imperial rule."

Other cheek

¹⁵"I tell you, Don't react violently against the one who is evil: when someone slaps you on the right cheek, turn the other as well."

Coat and shirt

¹⁶"If someone is determined to sue you for your coat, give that person the shirt off your back to go with it."

3:17

MATT 5:41
Source: Q

3:18

THOM 39:3; MATT 10:16
Sources: Matthew, Thomas

3:19

THOM 42
Source: Thomas

3:20

LUKE 13:24
Matt 7:13–14
Source: Q

3:21–22

LUKE 12:58–59
Matt 5:25–26
Source: Q

4:1–2

MARK 1:21–22
Matt 7:28–29; Luke 4:31–32
Source: Mark

Second mile

¹⁷"When anyone conscripts you for one mile of service, go along a second mile."

Sly as snakes

¹⁸Jesus would advise them, "Be as sly as snakes and as simple as doves."

Passersby

¹⁹Jesus used to recommend, "Be passersby."

Narrow door

²⁰Jesus would say, "Struggle to get in through the narrow door; I'm telling you, many will try to get in, but won't be able."

Before the judge

²¹Jesus said, "When you are about to appear with your opponent before the magistrate, do your best to settle with him on the way, or else he might drag you up before the judge, and the judge turn you over to the jailer, and the jailer throw you into prison. ²²I tell you, you'll never get out of there until you've paid every last red cent."

4   *Teaching with authority*

In the synagogue at Capernaum

Then they come to Capernaum, and on the sabbath day he went right to the synagogue and started teaching. ²They were astonished at his teaching, since he would teach them on his own authority, unlike the scholars.

4:3
MATT 20:16
Mark 10:31; Matt 19:30; Luke 13:30; Thom 4:2–3
Sources: Q Thomas, Mark

4:4–21
MATT 20:1–15
Source: Matthew

Reversal of expectations

First and last
³Jesus said, "The last will be first and the first last."

Vineyard laborers
⁴Jesus used to tell this parable:

⁵Heaven's imperial rule is like a proprietor who went out the first thing in the morning to hire workers for his vineyard. ⁶After agreeing with the workers for a silver coin a day, he sent them into his vineyard.

⁷And coming out around nine A.M., he saw others loitering in the marketplace ⁸and he said to them, "You go into the vineyard too, and I'll pay you whatever is fair." ⁹So they went.

¹⁰Around noon he went out again, and at three P.M. he repeated the process. ¹¹About five P.M. he went out and found others loitering about and says to them, "Why did you stand around here idle the whole day?"

¹²They reply, "Because no one hired us."

¹³He tells them, "You go into the vineyard as well."

¹⁴When evening came, the owner of the vineyard tells his foreman: "Call the workers and pay them their wages, starting with those hired last and ending with those hired first."

¹⁵Those hired at five P.M. came up and received a silver coin each. ¹⁶Those hired first approached, thinking they would receive more. But they also got a silver coin apiece. ¹⁷They took it and began to grumble against the proprietor: "These guys hired last worked only an hour but you have made them equal to us who did most of the work during the heat of the day."

¹⁸In response he said to one of them, "Look, pal, did I wrong you? You did agree with me for a silver coin, didn't you? ¹⁹Take your wage and get out! I intend to

4:22–23
THOM 41:1–2
Mark 4:25; Luke 8:18; Matt 13:12, 25:29; Luke 19:26
Sources: Thomas, Mark, Q

4:24–38
MATT 25:14–28
Luke 19:12–24
Source: Q

treat the one hired last the same way I treat you. ²⁰Is there some law forbidding me to do as I please with my money? ²¹Or is your eye filled with envy because I am generous?"

Have and have not
²²Jesus used to say: "Those who have something in hand will be given more, ²³and those who have nothing will be deprived of even the little they have."

Money in trust
²⁴Jesus would tell this parable:

You know, it's like a man going on a trip who called his slaves and turned his valuables over to them. ²⁵To the first he gave thirty thousand silver coins, to the second twelve thousand, and to the third six thousand, to each in relation to his ability, and he left.

²⁶Immediately the one who had received thirty thousand silver coins went out and put the money to work; he doubled his investment.

²⁷The second also doubled his money.

²⁸But the third, who had received the smallest amount, went out, dug a hole, and hid his master's silver.

²⁹After a long absence, the slaves' master returned to settle accounts with them. ³⁰The first, who had received thirty thousand silver coins, came and produced an additional thirty thousand, with this report: "Master, you handed me thirty thousand silver coins; as you can see, I have made you another thirty thousand."

³¹His master commended him: "Well done, you competent and reliable slave! You have been trustworthy in small amounts; I'll put you in charge of large amounts."

³²The one with twelve thousand silver coins also came and reported: "Master, you handed me twelve thousand

5:1–5
MARK 1:35–39
Luke 4:42–44
Source: Mark

silver coins; as you can see, I have made you another twelve thousand."

³³His master commended him: "Well done, you competent and reliable slave! You have been trustworthy in small amounts; I'll put you in charge of large amounts."

³⁴The one who had received six thousand silver coins also came and reported: "Master, I know that you drive a hard bargain, reaping where you didn't sow and gathering where you didn't scatter. ³⁵Since I was afraid, I went out and buried your money in the ground. Look, here it is!"

³⁶But his master replied to him, "You incompetent and timid slave! So you knew that I reap where I didn't sow and gather where I didn't scatter, did you? ³⁷Then you should have taken my money to the bankers. Then when I returned I would have received my capital with interest. ³⁸So take the money away from this fellow and give it to the one who has the greatest sum."

5   *Demons by the finger of God*

Jesus tours Galilee

Rising early, while it was still very dark, he went outside and stole away to an isolated place, where he started praying. ²Then Simon and those with him hunted him down. ³When they had found him they say to him, "Everybody's looking for you."

⁴But he replies: "Let's go somewhere else, to the neighboring villages, so I can speak there too, since that's what I'm here for."

⁵So he went all around Galilee speaking in their synagogues and driving out demons.

5:6–11
MARK 1:23–28
Luke 4:33–37
Source: Mark

5:12–16
LUKE 11:15–19
Mark 3:22–26; Matt 12:24–27
Sources: Q, Mark

5:17
LUKE 11:20
Matt 12:28
Source: Q

Unclean demon

⁶Now right there in their synagogue was a person possessed by an unclean spirit, which shouted, ⁷"Jesus! What do you want with us, you Nazarene? Have you come to get rid of us? I know you, who you are: God's holy man!"

⁸But Jesus yelled at it, "Shut up and get out of him!"

⁹Then the unclean spirit threw the man into convulsions, and letting out a loud shriek it came out of him. ¹⁰And they were all so amazed that they asked themselves, "What's this? A new kind of teaching backed by authority! He gives orders even to unclean spirits and they obey him!"

¹¹So his fame spread rapidly everywhere throughout Galilee and even beyond.

Beelzebul controversy

¹²And some in the crowds around Jesus would say, "He drives out demons in the name of Beelzebul, the head demon." ¹³Others were testing him by demanding a sign from heaven. ¹⁴But he knew what they were thinking, and said to them: "Every government divided against itself is devastated, and a house divided against a house falls. ¹⁵If Satan is divided against himself—since you claim I drive out demons in Beelzebul's name—how will his domain endure? ¹⁶If I drive out demons in Beelzebul's name, in whose name do your own people drive them out? In that case, they will be your judges."

Demons by the finger of God

¹⁷Jesus said, "But if by God's finger I drive out demons, then for you God's imperial rule has arrived."

5:18

5:19

5:20

5:21–28

5:29–31

Powerful man

18"No one can enter a powerful man's house to steal his belongings unless he first ties him up. Only then does he loot his house."

Satan's fall

19Jesus said to them, "I was watching Satan fall like lightning from heaven."

Fire on earth

20Jesus said, "I have cast fire upon the world, and look, I'm guarding it until it blazes."

Greek woman's daughter

21From there he got up and went away to the regions of Tyre. Whenever he visited a house he wanted no one to know, but he could not escape notice. 22Instead, suddenly a woman whose daughter had an unclean spirit heard about him, and came and fell down at his feet. 23The woman was a Greek, by race a Phoenician from Syria. 24And she started asking him to drive the demon out of her daughter. 25He responded to her like this: "Let the children be fed first, since it isn't good to take bread out of children's mouths and throw it to the dogs!"

26But as a rejoinder she says to him, "Sir, even the dogs under the table get to eat scraps dropped by children!"

27Then he said to her, "For that retort, be on your way, the demon has come out of your daughter."

28She returned home and found the child lying on the bed and the demon gone.

Return of an unclean spirit

29Jesus said, "When an unclean spirit leaves a person, it wanders through waterless places in search of a resting place. When it doesn't find one, it says, 'I will go back to

6:1–12
MARK 6:14–29
Matt 14:1–12
Source: Mark

the home I left.' ³⁰It then returns, and finds it swept and refurbished. ³¹Next, it goes out and brings back seven other spirits more vile than itself, who enter and settle in there. So that person ends up worse off than when he or she started."

6 *Death of John the Baptist*

Herod beheads John the Baptist

King Herod heard about Jesus' exorcism and cures—by now, Jesus' reputation had become well known. ²Some spread the rumor that he was Elijah, while others reported that he was a prophet like one of the prophets.

³Earlier, Herod himself had sent someone to arrest John and put him in chains in a dungeon, on account of Herodias, because he had abandoned his first wife and married her. ⁴So Herodias nursed a grudge against him and wanted to eliminate him, but she couldn't manage it, ⁵because Herod was afraid of John.

⁶Now a festival day came, when Herod gave a banquet on his birthday for his courtiers, and his commanders, and the leading citizens of Galilee. ⁷And the daughter of Herodias came in and captivated Herod and his dinner guests by dancing. ⁸The king said to the girl, "Ask me for whatever you wish and I'll grant it to you!" ⁹Then he swore an oath to her: "I'll grant you whatever you ask for, up to half my domain!"

¹⁰She promptly made her request: "I want you to give me the head of John the Baptist on a platter, right now!"

¹¹The king grew regretful, but, on account of his oaths and the dinner guests, he didn't want to refuse her. ¹²So right away the king sent for the executioner and commanded him to bring his head. And he went away and beheaded John in prison.

Into the wilderness

¹³Jesus began to talk about John to the crowds: "What did you go out to the wilderness to gawk at? A reed shaking in the wind? ¹⁴What did you really go out to see? A man dressed in fancy clothes? But wait! Those who wear fancy clothes are found in regal quarters."

7 *Love & forgiveness*

Teaching by the sea

Again he went out by the sea. And, with a huge crowd gathered around him, he started teaching.

Love, reciprocity and forgiveness

Love of enemies

²"To you who are listening I say, love your enemies. ³If you love those who love you, what merit is there in that? After all, even sinners love those who love them. ⁴And if you do good to those who do good to you, what merit is there in that? After all, even sinners do as much."

Sun and rain

⁵Jesus said, "God causes the sun to rise on both the bad and the good, and sends rain on both the just and the unjust. As you know, God is generous to the ungrateful and the wicked."

Reciprocity

⁶Jesus said, "Forgive and you'll be forgiven."

Forgive our debts

⁷"Father, forgive our debts to the extent we have forgiven those in debt to us."

7:8–19
MATT 18:23–34
Source: Matthew

7:20–30
JOHN 8:3–11
Source: fragment of an unknown gospel

Unforgiving slave

[8]"This is why Heaven's imperial rule should be compared to a secular ruler who decided to settle accounts with his slaves. [9]When the process began, this debtor was brought to him who owed ten million dollars. [10]Since he couldn't pay it back, the ruler ordered him sold, along with his wife and children and everything he had, so he could recover his money.

[11]"At this prospect, the slave fell down and groveled before him: 'Be patient with me, and I'll repay every cent.' [12]Because he was compassionate, the master of that slave let him go and canceled the debt.

[13]"As soon as he got out, that same fellow collared one of his fellow slaves who owed him a hundred dollars, and grabbed him by the neck and demanded: 'Pay back what you owe!'

[14]"His fellow slave fell down and begged him: 'Be patient with me and I'll pay you back.'

[15]"But he wasn't interested; instead, he went out and threw him in prison until he paid the debt.

[16]"When his fellow slaves realized what had happened, they were terribly distressed and went and reported to their master everything that had taken place.

[17]"At that point, his master summoned him: 'You wicked slave,' he says to him, 'I canceled your entire debt because you begged me. [18]Wasn't it only fair for you to treat your fellow slave with the same consideration as I treated you?' [19]And the master was so angry he handed him over to those in charge of punishment until he paid back everything he owed."

The first stone

[20]The scholars and members of the purity party bring him a woman who was caught committing adultery. They make her stand there in front of everybody, [21]and

they address Jesus, "Teacher, this woman was caught in the act of adultery. ²²In the Law Moses commanded us to stone women like this. What do you say?" ²³(They said this to trap him, so they would have something to accuse him of.)

²⁴Jesus stooped down and began drawing on the ground with his finger. ²⁵When they insisted on an answer, he stood up and replied, "Whoever in this crowd has never committed a sin should go ahead and throw the first stone at her." ²⁶Once again he squatted down and continued writing on the ground.

²⁷His audience began to drift away, one by one—the elders were the first to go—until Jesus was the only one left, with the woman there in front of him.

²⁸Jesus stood up and said to her, "Woman, where is everybody? Hasn't anyone condemned you?"

²⁹She replied, "No one, sir."

³⁰"I don't condemn you, either," Jesus said. "You're free to go, but from now on no more sinning."

8 *Jesus at the table*

Dining with sinners

On one occasion Jesus happens to recline at table, along with many toll collectors and sinners. ²(Remember, there were many of these people and they were all following him.) ³And whenever the Pharisees' scholars saw him eating with sinners and toll collectors, they would raise the question: "What's he doing eating with toll collectors and sinners?"

⁴Jesus responds, "Since when do the able-bodied need a doctor? It's the sick who do. ⁵I did not come to enlist religious folks but sinners!"

8:6–7
LUKE 15:1–2
Source: Luke

8:8–9
MARK 2:18–19
Matt 9:14–15; Luke 5:33–34
Source: Mark

8:10–11
THOM 47:3–4
Luke 5:37–39; Mark 2:22; Matt 9:17
Sources: Thomas, Luke, Mark, common lore

9:1–5
LUKE 7:31–35
Matt 11:16–19
Source: Q

⁶Now the toll collectors and sinners kept crowding around Jesus so they could hear him. ⁷But the Pharisees and the scholars would complain to each other, "This fellow welcomes sinners and eats with them."

Question of fasting

⁸John's disciples and the Pharisees were in the habit of fasting, and they come and ask him, "Why do the disciples of John fast, and the disciples of the Pharisees, but your disciples don't?"

⁹And Jesus said to them, "The groom's friends can't fast while the groom is around, can they? So long as the groom is around, you can't expect them to fast."

Aged wine

¹⁰Jesus said, "Nobody drinks aged wine and immediately wants to drink young wine. ¹¹Young wine is not poured into old wineskins, or they might break, and aged wine is not poured into a new wineskin, or it might spoil."

9   *Celebration*

Children in the marketplace

"What do members of this generation remind me of? What are they like? ²They are like children sitting in the marketplace and calling out to one another:

> We played the flute for you,
> but you wouldn't dance;
> we sang a dirge,
> but you wouldn't weep.

³"Just remember, John the Baptist appeared on the scene, eating no bread and drinking no wine, and you say, 'He is demented.' ⁴This mother's son appeared on the scene both eating and drinking, and you say, 'There's a glutton and a drunk, a crony of toll collectors and sinners!' ⁵Indeed, wisdom is vindicated by all her children."

Lost coin

⁶Jesus asked this question: "Is there any woman with ten silver coins, who if she loses one, wouldn't light a lamp and sweep the house and search carefully until she finds it? ⁷When she finds it, she invites her friends and neighbors over and says, 'Celebrate with me, because I have found the silver coin I had lost.'"

Lost sheep

Jesus told them this parable:

⁸Suppose one of you owns a hundred sheep and one of them strays off. You would leave the ninety-nine behind in the wilderness and go search for the one that was lost, wouldn't you? ⁹And when you find it, you would lift it up on your shoulders, happy, wouldn't you? ¹⁰Once you get home, you would invite your friends and neighbors over, and say to them, "Celebrate with me, because I have found my lost sheep."

Cache of coins

¹¹Jesus said, "Heaven's imperial rule is like treasure hidden in a field: when someone finds it, that person covers it up again, ¹²and out of sheer joy goes and sells every last possession and buys that field."

Pearl

¹³Jesus said, "The Father's imperial rule is like a merchant who had a supply of merchandise and then found

9:15–46
LUKE 15:11–32
Source: Luke

a pearl. ¹⁴That merchant was prudent; he sold the merchandise and bought the single pearl for himself."

Prodigal

¹⁵On another occasion, he told this parable:

¹⁶Once there was a fellow who had two sons. ¹⁷The younger of them said to his father, "Father, give me the share of the property that is coming to me." ¹⁸So the Father divided the estate between the two boys.

¹⁹Not long after that, the younger son gathered his belongings together and departed for a distant country, where he squandered his inheritance by living extravagantly. ²⁰Just as he began to run out of funds, a severe famine swept through the land and he had to do without. ²¹So he went and hired himself out to one of the citizens of that country, who sent him out to his farm to feed the pigs. ²²He was reduced to satisfying his hunger with eating pig's food because no one gave him anything to eat.

²³He finally came to his senses and said to himself, "Lots of my father's hired hands have plenty to eat while I am dying of starvation! ²⁴I'll return to my father and I'll tell him, 'Father, I have sinned against God and I have wronged you. ²⁵I don't deserve to be called your son. Treat me like one of your hired hands.'" ²⁶And he acted on his resolve and returned to his father.

²⁷His father saw him coming while he was still some distance off and his heart went out to his son. ²⁸He went running out to meet him, threw his arms around his neck, and kissed him. ²⁹And the son said to him, "Father, I have sinned against God and I have wronged you. ³⁰I don't deserve to be called your son. Treat me like one of your hired hands."

³¹His father commanded his slaves, "Quick! Get our finest robe and put it on him; provide him with a ring for

10:1–4
MARK 2:23–24, 27–28
Matt 12:1–2, 8; Luke 6:1–2, 5
Source: Mark

his finger and sandals for his feet. ³²Fetch the fat calf and slaughter it. Let's have a feast and celebrate. ³³After all, this son of mine was dead but has come back to life; he was lost but now has been found." ³⁴And they started to celebrate.

³⁵Now the older son was out in the field at the time, ³⁶but as he got closer to the house, he heard music and dancing. ³⁷He called one of the servant boys over and asked him what was going on.

³⁸The boy told him, "Your brother has come home and your father has slaughtered the fat calf because he has come back safe and sound."

³⁹The older son was angry and refused to enter the house. ⁴⁰So his father came out and began to plead with him. ⁴¹But he said to his father, "See here, all these years I have slaved for you. I never once disobeyed your orders. ⁴²Yet you have never once provided me with so much as a kid goat so I could celebrate with my friends. ⁴³But when this son of yours shows up—the one who squandered your fortune with prostitutes—for him you slaughter the fat calf."

⁴⁴To his son the father replied, "My child, you are always at my side. ⁴⁵Everything that's mine is yours. ⁴⁶But we just had to celebrate and rejoice because this brother of yours was dead but has come back to life; he was lost but now has been found."

10 *Sabbath observance*

Lord of the sabbath

It so happened that Jesus was walking along through the grainfields on the sabbath day, and his disciples began to strip heads of grain as they walked along. ²And

10:5–11
MARK 3:1–5
Matt 12:9–13; Luke 6:6–10
Source: Mark

11:1–3
MARK 3:20–21
Source: Mark

11:4
JOHN 10:20
Source: John

the Pharisees started to argue with him: "See here, why are they doing what's not permitted on the sabbath day?"

³And Jesus says to them:

The sabbath day was created for Adam and Eve,
not Adam and Eve for the sabbath day.
⁴So, the son of Adam lords it even over the sabbath
day.

Man with crippled hand

⁵Then he went back to the synagogue, and a fellow with a crippled hand was there. ⁶So they kept an eye on him, to see whether he would heal the fellow on the sabbath day, so they could denounce him. ⁷And he says to the fellow with the crippled hand, "Get up here in front of everybody." ⁸Then he asks them, "On the sabbath day is it permitted to do good or to do evil, to save life or to destroy it?"

⁹But they maintained their silence. ¹⁰And looking right at them with anger, exasperated at their obstinacy, he says to the fellow, "Hold out your hand!"

¹¹He held it out and his hand was restored.

11 *Kinship in the kingdom*

Jesus' relatives think him mad

Then he goes home, and once again a crowd gathers, so they could not even grab a bite to eat. ²When his relatives heard about it, they came to get him. ³(You see, they thought he was out of his mind.) ⁴Many folks were saying, "He's out of his mind and crazy. Why pay attention to him?"

True relatives

⁵Then his mother and his brothers arrive. While still outside, they send in and ask for him. ⁶A crowd was sitting around him, and they say to him, "Look, your mother and your brothers and sisters are outside looking for you."

⁷In response he says to them: "My mother and brothers—who ever are they?"

⁸And looking right at those seated around him in a circle, he says, "Here are my mother and my brothers. ⁹Whoever does God's will, that's my brother and sister and mother!"

Hating father and mother

¹⁰Once when hordes of people were traveling with him, he turned and addressed them: ¹¹"If any of you comes to me and does not hate your own father and mother and wife and children and brothers and sisters— yes, even your own life—you're no disciple of mine."

No respect at home

¹²Then he left that place, and he comes to his hometown, and his disciples follow him. ¹³When the sabbath day arrived, he started teaching in the synagogue; and many who heard him were astounded and said so: "Where's he getting this?" and "What's the source of all this wisdom?" and ¹⁴"Who gave him the right to perform such miracles? ¹⁵This is the carpenter, isn't it? Isn't he Mary's son? And who are his brothers, if not James and Judas and Simon? And who are his sisters, if not our neighbors?" ¹⁶And they were resentful of him.

¹⁷Jesus used to tell them: "No prophet goes without respect, except on his home turf and among his relatives and at home!"

¹⁸He was unable to perform a single miracle there, except that he did cure a few by laying hands on them. ¹⁹And he used to go around the villages, teaching them.

12 *In parables*

Teaching by the sea

Once again he started to teach beside the sea. ²An enormous crowd gathers around him, so he climbs into a boat and sits there on the water facing the huge crowd on the shore.

³He would teach them many things in parables.

Sower

⁴Jesus said, "Listen to this! This sower went out to sow. ⁵While he was sowing, some seed fell along the path, and the birds came and ate it up. ⁶Other seed fell on rocky ground where there wasn't much soil, and it came up right away because the soil had no depth. ⁷But when the sun came up it was scorched, and because it had no root it withered. ⁸Still other seed fell among thorns, and the thorns came up and choked it, so that it produced no fruit. ⁹Finally, some seed fell on good earth and started producing fruit. The seed sprouted and grew: one part had a yield of thirty, another part sixty, and a third part one hundred."

Seed and harvest

¹⁰Jesus would say, "God's imperial rule is like this:

Suppose someone sows seed on the ground, ¹¹and goes to bed and gets up day after day, and the seed sprouts and matures, although the sower is unaware of it. ¹²The earth produces fruit on its own, first a shoot,

12:14–26
LUKE 16:1-8
Source: Luke

12:27–31
LUKE 18:2–5
Source: Luke

then a head, then mature grain on the head. ¹³But when the grain ripens, all of a sudden that farmer sends for the sickle , because it's harvest time."

Shrewd manager

¹⁴Jesus used to tell this story to his disciples:

¹⁵There was this rich man whose manager had been accused of squandering his master's property. ¹⁶He called him in and said, "What's this I hear about you? Let's have an audit of your management, because your job is being terminated."

¹⁷Then the manager said to himself, "What am I going to do? My master is firing me. I'm not able to dig ditches and I'm ashamed to beg. ¹⁸I've got it! I know what I'll do so doors will open for me when I'm removed from management."

¹⁹So he called in each of his master's debtors. He said to the first, "How much do you owe my master?"

²⁰He said, "Five hundred gallons of olive oil."

²¹And he said to him, "Here is your invoice; sit down right now and make it two hundred and fifty."

²²Then he said to another, "And how much do you owe?"

²³He said, "A thousand bushels of wheat."

²⁴He says to him, "Here is your invoice; make it eight hundred."

²⁵The master praised the dishonest manager because he had acted shrewdly; ²⁶for the children of this world exhibit better sense in dealing with their own kind than do the children of light.

Corrupt judge

²⁷He told them a parable:

²⁸Once there was a judge in this town who neither feared God nor cared about people.

12:32–38
THOM 65:1–7
Mark 12:1–8; Matt 21:33–39; Luke 20:9–15
Sources: Thomas, Mark

12:39–41
THOM 98:1–3
Source: Thomas

²⁹In that same town was a widow who kept coming to him and demanding, "Give me a ruling against the person I'm suing."

³⁰For a while he refused; but eventually he said to himself, "I'm not afraid of God and I don't care about people, ³¹but this widow keeps pestering me. So I'm going to give her a favorable ruling, or else she'll keep coming back until she wears me down."

Leased vineyard

³²Jesus told this parable:

A person owned a vineyard and rented it to some farmers, so they could work it and he could collect its crop from them. ³³He sent his slave so the farmers would give him the vineyard's crop. ³⁴They grabbed him, beat him, and almost killed him, and the slave returned and told his master. ³⁵His master said, "Perhaps he didn't know them." ³⁶He sent another slave, and the farmers beat that one as well. ³⁷Then the master sent his son and said, "Perhaps they'll show my son some respect." ³⁸Because the farmers knew that he was the heir to the vineyard, they grabbed him and killed him.

The assassin

³⁹Jesus would say, "The Father's imperial rule is like a person who wanted to kill someone powerful. ⁴⁰While still at home he drew his sword and thrust it into the wall to find out whether his hand would go in. ⁴¹Then he killed the powerful one."

13 *Public & private piety*

Closet prayer

Jesus said, "When you pray, go into a room by yourself and shut the door behind you."

Divine address

²"When you pray, say,
³Our Father,
⁴Your name be revered."

Pharisee and toll collector

⁵Jesus also told this parable:

⁶Two men went up to the temple to pray, one a Pharisee and the other a toll collector. ⁷The Pharisee stood up and prayed silently as follows: "I thank you, God, that I'm not like everybody else, thieving, unjust, adulterous, and especially not like that toll collector over there. ⁸I fast twice a week, I give tithes of everything that I acquire."

⁹But the toll collector stood off by himself and didn't even dare to look up, but struck his chest, and muttered, "God, have mercy on me, sinner that I am."

¹⁰Let me tell you, the second man went back home acquitted but the first one did not. For those who promote themselves will be demoted, but those who demote themselves will be promoted.

Sliver and timber

¹¹Jesus said, "You see the sliver in your friend's eye, but don't see the timber in your own eye. ¹²When you take the timber out of your own eye, then you will see well enough to remove the sliver from your friend's eye."

13:13

13:14–15

13:16

14:1–5

Veiled and unveiled

¹³Jesus said, "There is nothing veiled that won't be unveiled, or hidden that won't be made known."

Scholars' privileges

¹⁴Within earshot of the people Jesus said to the disciples, ¹⁵"Be on guard against the scholars who like to parade around in long robes, and who love to be addressed properly in the marketplace, and who prefer important seats in the synagogues and the best couches at banquets."

Left and right hands

¹⁶Jesus said, "When you give to charity, don't let your left hand know what your right hand is doing."

14 *Jesus & purity*

Eating with defiled hands

The Pharisees gather around him, along with some of the scholars, who had come from Jerusalem. ²When they notice some of his disciples eating their meal with defiled hands, that is to say, without washing their hands, ³the Pharisees and the scholars start questioning him: "Why don't your disciples live up to the tradition of the elders, instead of eating bread with defiled hands?" ⁴(Recall that the Pharisees and the Judeans generally wouldn't think of eating without first washing their hands in a particular way, always observing the tradition of the elders, ⁵and they won't eat when they get back from the marketplace without washing again, and there are many other traditions they cherish, such as the washing of cups and jugs and kettles.)

14:6–8
MARK 7:14–16
Thom 14:5; Matt 15:10–11
Sources: Mark, Thomas

14:9–10
THOM 89:1–2
Luke 11:39–40; Matt 23:25–26
Sources: Thomas, Q

15:1–3
MARK 8:11–13
Matt 16:1–4; 12:38–40; Luke 11:29–30
Cf. John 2:18; 6:30
Sources: Mark, Q

15:4–7
THOM 113:1–4
Source: Thomas

15:8–10
LUKE 17:20–21
Source: Q

What goes in

⁶As usual he summons a crowd and says to them, "Listen to me, all of you, and try to understand! ⁷What goes into you can't defile you; what comes out of you can. ⁸If anyone has two good ears, use them!"

Inside and outside

⁹Jesus said, "Why do you wash the outside of the cup? ¹⁰Don't you understand that the one who made the inside is also the one who made the outside?"

15   *Signs of God's imperial rule*

Demand for a sign

One time, some members of the Purity Party started to argue with him. To test him, they demanded a sign from heaven. ²He groaned under his breath and says, "Why does this generation insist on a sign? I swear to God, this generation won't get any sign!"

³And turning his back on them, he got back in the boat and crossed over to the other side.

The coming of God's imperial rule

⁴His disciples said to him, "When will the Father's imperial rule come?"

⁵"It will not come by watching for it. ⁶It will not be said, 'Look, here it is!' or 'Look, over there!' ⁷Rather, the Father's imperial rule is spread out upon the earth, and people don't see it."

⁸On another occasion Jesus said, "You won't be able to observe the coming of God's imperial rule. ⁹People are not going to be able to say, 'Look, here it is!' or 'Over

there!' ¹⁰On the contrary, God's imperial rule is right there in your presence."

Impose your rule

¹¹Jesus prayed, "Father, impose your imperial rule."

16 *Five cures*

Peter's mother-in-law

And when Jesus came to Peter's house, he noticed Peter's mother-in-law lying sick with a fever. ²He touched her hand and the fever disappeared. Then she got up and started looking after him.

Leper

³While Jesus was on tour, a leper comes up to him, pleads with him, falls down on his knees, and says to him, "If you want to, you can make me clean."

⁴Although Jesus was indignant, he stretched out his hand, touched him, and says to him, "Okay—you're clean!"

⁵And right away the leprosy disappeared, and he was made clean.

Paralytic and four

⁶Back again in Capernaum, the word got around that he was at home. ⁷And many people crowded around so there was no longer any room, even outside the door. Then he started speaking to them. ⁸Some people then show up with a paralytic being carried by four of them. ⁹And when they were not able to get near him on account of the crowd, they removed the roof above him. After digging it out, they lowered the mat on which the

16:16–19
MARK 5:24–34
Matt 9:20–22; Luke 8:43–48
Source: Mark

16:20–22
MARK 8:22–24
Source: Mark

paralytic was lying. [10]When Jesus noticed their trust, he says to the paralytic, "Child, your sins are forgiven."

[11]Some of the scholars were sitting there and silently wondering: [12]"Why does that fellow say such things? He's blaspheming! Who can forgive sins except the one God?"

[13]And right away, because Jesus sensed in his spirit that they were raising questions like this among themselves, he says to them: "Why do you entertain questions about these things? [14]Which is easier, to say to the paralytic, 'Your sins are forgiven,' or to say, 'Get up, pick up your mat and walk'?"

[15]And he got up, picked his mat right up, and walked out as everyone looked on. So they all became ecstatic, extolled God, and exclaimed, "We've never seen the likes of this!"

Woman with a vaginal hemorrhage

[16]On one occasion, a large crowd started following and shoving against Jesus. [17]In the crowd was a woman who had suffered from a vaginal hemorrhage. [18]When this woman heard about Jesus, she came up from behind in the crowd and touched his cloak. [19]And the vaginal flow stopped instantly, and she sensed in her body that she was cured of her illness.

Blind man of Bethsaida

[20]Jesus and his retinue come to Bethsaida, and they bring him a blind person, and plead with him to touch him. [21]He took the blind man by the hand and led him out of the village. And he spat into his eyes, and placed his hands on him, and started questioning him, "Do you see anything?"

[22]When his sight began to come back, the first thing he said was, "I see human figures, as though they were trees walking around."

17   *Success, wealth & God's domain*

The itinerant teacher

And from there he gets up and goes to the territory of Judea and across the Jordan, and once again crowds gather around him. As usual, he started teaching them.

Give to beggars

²Jesus advises, "Give to everyone who begs from you."

Lend without return

³Jesus said, "If you have money, don't lend it at interest. ⁴Rather, give it to someone from whom you won't get it back. ⁵If you lend to those from whom you hope to gain, what merit is there in that? Even sinners lend to sinners, in order to get as much in return."

Eye of the needle

⁶Jesus said to his disciples, "I swear to you, it is very difficult for the rich to enter Heaven's domain. ⁷And again I tell you, it's easier for a camel to squeeze through a needle's eye than for a wealthy person to get into God's domain."

Two masters

⁸Jesus said, "No servant can be a slave to two masters. No doubt that slave will either hate one and love the other, or be devoted to one and disdain the other. ⁹You can't be enslaved to both God and a bank account."

Rich farmer

¹⁰Jesus said, "There was a rich man who had a great deal of money. ¹¹He said, 'I shall invest my money so that

I may sow, reap, plant, and fill my storehouses with produce, that I may lack nothing.' [12]These were the things he was thinking in his heart, but that very night he died. [13]Anyone here with two ears had better listen!"

Saving one's life

[14]Jesus said, "Whoever tries to hang on to life will forfeit it, but whoever forfeits life will preserve it."

Castration for heaven

[15]Jesus said, "There are castrated men who were born that way, and there are castrated men who were castrated by others, and there are castrated men who castrated themselves because of Heaven's imperial rule."

18 *Hospitality*

Friend at midnight

Jesus said to them, "Suppose you have a friend who comes to you in the middle of the night and says to you, 'Friend, lend me three loaves, [2]for a friend of mine on a trip has just shown up and I have nothing to offer him.' [3]And suppose you reply, 'Stop bothering me. The door is already locked and my children and I are in bed. I can't get up to give you anything'—[4]I tell you, even though you won't get up and give the friend anything out of friendship, yet you will get up and give that person whatever is needed because you'd be ashamed not to."

Good gifts

[5]"Who among you would hand a son a stone when it's bread he's asking for? [6]Again, who would hand him a snake when it's fish he's asking for? Of course no one

would! [7]So if you, unscrupulous as you are, know how to give your children good gifts, isn't it much more likely that your Father in the heavens will give good things to those who ask him?"

Instructions for the road: house and food

[8]"Whenever you enter a house, first say, 'Peace to this house.' [9]Stay at that one house, eating and drinking whatever they provide. Do not move from house to house. [10]Whenever you enter a town and they welcome you, eat whatever is set before you."

Hospitable Samaritan

[11]"This guy was on his way down to Jericho from Jerusalem when he was waylaid by thieves. [12]They robbed him, beat him up, and ran off, leaving him for dead. [13]By chance a priest was on his way down that road; when he spied the victim, he went out of his way to avoid him. [14]Similarly, when a levite came to the place, he, too, took one look at him and passed by on the far side of the road. [15]In contrast, there was this Samaritan who was also traveling that way. [16]When he came to the place where the victim lay, he was moved to pity at the sight of him. He went up to him, treated his wounds with oil and wine, and bandaged them. [17]He hoisted the fellow onto his own animal, brought him to an inn, and cared for him. [18]The next day he took out two silver coins, which he gave to the innkeeper with these instructions, 'Look after him, and on my way back I'll reimburse you for any extra expense you've had.'"

19 *Sight & light*

Blind Bartimaeus

Then they come to Jericho. As he was leaving Jericho with his disciples and a sizable crowd, Bartimaeus, a blind beggar, the son of Timaeus, was sitting alongside the road. ²When he learned that it was Jesus the Nazarene, he began to shout: "You son of David, Jesus, have mercy on me!"

³And many kept yelling at him to shut up, but he shouted all the louder, "You son of David, have mercy on me!"

⁴Jesus paused and said, "Tell him to come over here!"

⁵They called to the blind man, "Be brave, get up, he's calling you!" ⁶So he threw off his cloak, and jumped to his feet, and went over to Jesus.

⁷In response Jesus said, "What do you want me to do for you?"

⁸The blind man said to him, "Rabbi, I want to see again!"

⁹And Jesus said to him, "Be on your way, your trust has cured you." ¹⁰And right away he regained his sight, and he started following him on the road.

Mountain city

¹¹"A city sitting on top of a mountain can't be concealed."

Lamp and bushel

¹²"People don't light a lamp and put it under a bushel basket but rather on a lampstand, where it sheds light for everyone in the house."

By their fruit

¹³"You'll know who folks are by what they produce. Since when do people pick grapes from thorns or figs from thistles?"

Fig tree without figs

¹⁴Then he told this parable:

A man had a fig tree growing in his vineyard; he came looking for fruit on it but didn't find any.

¹⁵So he said to the vinekeeper, "See here, for three years in a row I have come looking for fruit on this tree, and haven't found any. Cut it down. Why should it suck the nutrients out of the soil?"

¹⁶In response he says to him, "Let it stand, sir, one more year, until I get a chance to dig around it and work in some manure. ¹⁷Maybe it will produce next year; but if it doesn't, we can go ahead and cut it down."

Saltless salt

¹⁸"Salt is good and salty, but if it becomes bland—loses its zing—with what will you renew it?"

20 *In Jerusalem*

Temple incident

They come to Jerusalem. And he went into the temple and began chasing the vendors and shoppers out of the temple area, and he turned the bankers' tables upside down, along with the chairs of the pigeon merchants. ²Then he started teaching and would say to them: "Don't the scriptures say, 'My house is to be regarded as a house of prayer for all peoples'?—but you have turned it into 'a hideout for crooks'!"

20:3–4

THOM 100:1–3

Mark 12:13–17; Matt 22:15–22; Luke 20:21; EgerG 3:1–6

Sources: Mark, Thomas, Egerton Gospel

20:5–11

JOHN 5:2–3, 5–9

Source: John

21:1

MARK 14:43

Matt 26:47; Luke 22:47

Source: Mark

21:2

JOHN 18:1–2

Source: John

21:3

MARK 14:46

Matt 26:50; Luke 22:54; John 18:12

Sources: Mark, John

21:4

MARK 14:50

Matt 26:56

Source: Mark

21:5

MARK 14:53

Matt 26:57; Luke 22:54; John 18:13

Sources: Mark, John

Emperor and God

³They showed Jesus a gold coin and said to him, "The Roman emperor's people demand taxes from us."

⁴He said to them, "Give the emperor what belongs to the emperor, and give God what belongs to God."

Paralytic by the pool

⁵In Jerusalem, by the Sheep Gate, there is a pool, called Bethzatha in Hebrew. It has five colonnades, ⁶among which numerous invalids were usually lying around—blind, lame, paralyzed. ⁷One man had been crippled for thirty-eight years. ⁸Jesus observed him lying there and realized he had been there a long time.

"Do you want to get well?" he asks him.

⁹The crippled man replied, "Sir, I don't have anyone to put me in the pool when the water is agitated; while I'm trying to get in someone else beats me to it."

¹⁰"Get up, pick up your mat and start walking around," Jesus tells him.

¹¹And at once the man recovered; he picked up his mat and began walking.

21 *The passion*

The arrest

Led by one of Jesus' disciples, the police show up at the place Jesus and the rest of his followers were gathered. ²Because Jesus had often gone to the place, Jesus' followers knew the place too. ³And the police seized Jesus and held him fast. ⁴And the disciples all deserted Jesus and ran away.

Before the high priest

⁵They brought Jesus before the high priest.

21:6–7

MARK 15:1, 15

Matt, 27:1–2; 26; Luke 23:1; John 18:28, 19:1, 16

Sources: Mark, John

21:8–9

MARK 15:22, 24

Matt 27:33, 35; Luke 23:33; John 19:17–18

Sources: Mark, John

21:10–11

MARK 15:40–41

Matt 27:55–56; Luke 23:49; John 19:25

Sources: Mark, John

21:12

MARK 15:37

Matt 27:50; Luke 23:46; John 19:30

Sources: Mark, John

Before Pilate

[6]The ranking priests bound Jesus and turned him over to Pilate, the Roman governor.

[7]Then Pilate had Jesus flogged and turned him over to be crucified.

The crucifixion

[8]And the Roman soldiers bring him to the place Golgotha (which means "Place of the skull"). [9]And the soldiers crucify him.

[10]Now some women were observing this from a distance, among whom were Mary of Magdala, and Mary the mother of James the younger and Joses, and Salome. [11]These women had regularly followed and assisted him when he was in Galilee, along with many other women who had come up to Jerusalem in his company.

The death

[12]Then Jesus breathed his last.

v. 1–3
PSMARK 16:9–11
Matt 28:9–10; John 20:1–2; 11–18
Sources: PseudoMark, Matthew, John

v. 4
1 COR 15:5; LUKE 24:34
Sources: Paul, Luke

v. 5
1 COR 15:8
Cf. Acts 9:3–19; 22:1–16; 26:9–18
Sources: Paul, Luke

v. 6
MARY 7:1; MATT 28:9–10; JOHN 20:11–18; PSMARK 16:9–11
Sources: Gospel of Mary, Matthew, John, Pseudo-Mark

vv. 7–8
GAL 2:7, 9
Source: Paul

Pillars & pioneers

Appearance to Mary of Magdala

Jesus appeared first to Mary of Magdala, from whom he had driven out seven demons. ²She went and told those who were close to him, who were mourning and weeping. ³But when those folks heard that he was alive and had been seen by her, they did not believe it.

Appearance to Peter

⁴Christ appeared to Cephas (Peter).

Appearance to Paul

⁵"Last of all, like the freak of nature I am, Christ appeared to me as well."

Mary's Vision

⁶Mary of Magdala said, "I saw the Lord in a vision, and I said to him, 'Lord, I saw you today in a vision.'"

Pillars of the Jerusalem Community

⁷James, the Lord's brother, and Cephas (Peter), and John, the son of Zebedee, were pillars of the Jerusalem community.

Gospel for the Jews and Gentiles

⁸"They agreed that I, Paul, had been entrusted with the gospel to the uncircumcised, just as Cephas had been entrusted with the gospel to the circumcised."

Abbreviations

Acts	Acts of the Apostles
B.C.E.	Before the Common Era
C.E.	Common Era
col.	column
1–2 Cor	1–2 Corinthians
EgerG	Egerton Gospel
epil	epilogue
Gal	Galatians
GJes	Gospel of Jesus
GosFr 1224	Papyrus Oxyrhynchus 1224
John	Gospel of John
Luke	Gospel of Luke
Mark	Gospel of Mark
Mary	Gospel of Mary
Matt	Gospel of Matthew
prol	prologue
PsMark	Pseudo-Mark (Mark 16:9–20)
Q	Sayings in Gospel Q
Thom	Gospel of Thomas
v.	verse

References

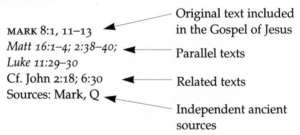

MARK 8:1, 11–13 — Original text included in the Gospel of Jesus

Matt 16:1–4; 2:38–40;
Luke 11:29–30 — Parallel texts

Cf. John 2:18; 6:30 — Related texts

Sources: Mark, Q — Independent ancient sources

Birth, childhood, and family of Jesus

prol 1
MATT 1:1;
LUKE 3:34

In popular piety, all Judeans were descendants of Abraham, the father of the race. There is no reason to believe that records existed to verify the actual ancestors of Jesus. The genealogies of Jesus are therefore fiction that attempt to provide Jesus with illustrious royal ancestors.

prol 2
MATT 1:16;
LUKE 1:27

Outside the birth and childhood stories in Matthew (chaps. 1–2) and Luke (chaps. 1–2, 3:23–38), Mary is mentioned in the New Testament only in Mark 6:3, in the parallel Matt 13:55, and Acts 1:14. Joseph is mentioned as Jesus' father only in Luke 4:22, John 1:45, and 6:42, again outside the birth and child-hood stories of Matthew and Luke.

prol 3
MATT 2:1;
LUKE 1:5

Herod the Great died in 4 B.C.E.

prol 4
LUKE 2:21;
MATT 1:25

Jesus was probably circumcised in accordance with Jewish practice. Jesus is his Greek name, Yeshua his Aramaic name. The name may be the most reliable piece of information we have about the sage from Nazareth. We have no other reliable information about Jesus' child-hood. Legends that Jesus visited India and Tiber during his youth are all late and without historical foundation.

prol 5
MARK 6:3

Jesus may have adopted the vocation of Joseph, who was a woodworker or artisan. In Mark 6:3, Jesus is referred to as a *tekton*, often translated as carpenter. Matthew (13:55) changes this to *tekton's* son. A woodworker was an artisan, which placed Jesus or Jesus' father at the bottom of the economic ladder. More generally, Jesus belonged to the peasant class and may have engaged in farming since his parables draw frequently on images from agriculture.

prol 6
MARK 6:3

That Jesus was known as Mary's son suggests some aberration in his birth. The customary way to identify a son was in relation to the father.

prol 7
MARK 6:3

Jesus' family included three or four brothers as well as unnamed sisters. Matthew (13:55) adds the name of Joseph or Joses as the fourth brother. According to Paul (1 Cor 9:5), the brothers of Jesus were married.

prol 8–9
JOHN 1:45–46

Jesus is often identified by his hometown Nazareth. He is never identified by Bethlehem, his alleged birthplace. This suggests that Jesus was actually born in Nazareth, contrary to the claim of the legendary birth stories.

prol 10–12
MARK 3:21;
MATT 13:57

Jesus' brothers and sisters were apparently not in sympathy with his cause during his lifetime.

prol 13–14

According to Paul, Jesus' brother James later became a leader in the Jerusalem congregation. He was known as a "pillar" along with Simon Peter (Cephas) and John.

prol 15
1 COR 15:7

According to Paul, James claimed a revelatory vision or experience of Jesus after Jesus' death. James was probably martyred in 62 C.E. in Jerusalem (Josephus, *Antiquities of the Jews* 20.9.1; Eusebuis, *Ecclesiastical History* 2.23.1–18, quoting Hegesippus). The family of Jesus later played a central role in the leadership of the early Jerusalem community (Eusebius, *Ecclesiastical History* 3.11.1; 3.19.1–20.7, again quoting Hegesippus).

John the Baptist and Jesus

1:1–3
MARK 1:4–6

The claim that John wore a camel hair mantel and had a leather girdle about his waist recalls the description of Elijah in 2 Kings 1:8 and corresponds to the depiction of a prophet's attire in Zech 13:4. For that reason, the Fellows were skeptical about this piece of information and colored it gray.

1:4
MATT 3:1–2
This statement probably accurately summarizes the preaching of John. However, Mark ascribes the same message to Jesus (1:15). See the note on 2:1 for the reasons the Fellows think the ascription here is correct.

1:5–14
LUKE 3:7–15
Much of the discourse attributed to John was colored gray by the Fellows as words that probably reflect John's preaching but which would not have been remembered in detail. Gray was therefore the correct choice.

1:15–16
MARK 1:7–8
John the Baptist did anticipate the arrival of a messiah who would succeed him, but it is doubtful that he compared his own water baptism with a future spirit baptism. That sounds like a Christian touch. The Fellows colored v. 16 gray.

1:21–31
MATT 4:1–11
The Fellows of the Jesus Seminar voted the core of the temptation story gray rather than black on the grounds that Jesus may have undergone some sort of vision quest in the desert. However, they regarded the specific content of this story as a fiction. The devil and Satan are of course mythic figures. Although fictive, the story contains some interesting points. Jesus is represented as rejecting the miraculous approach to messiahship and as refusing to supply bread to the hungry as the means of winning approval. Yet both the gospels of Matthew and Luke, in following the Sayings Gospel Q, depict Jesus as doing both of these things in the course of his public ministry. The temptation story is thus a kind of counterweight to the feeding of the multitudes and the nature wonders.

Jesus announces the good news

2:1
MARK 1:14

Not a apocalyptic prophet N·

According to Mark 1:15, Jesus proclaims that God's imperial rule is at hand, he calls on people to undergo a change of heart, and he invites them to put their trust in the good news. The Fellows voted this summary black as the work of Mark, who borrowed the content from the preaching of John the Baptist. It is more accurate to present the authentic beatitudes as a summary of the gospel of Jesus than to have Jesus echo the message of John. The Jesus Seminar became convinced that Jesus was not an apocalyptic prophet like John, because many of his parables and many of his aphorisms do not portray him as anticipating imminent divine judgment.

2:6–8
MARK 10:13–15

Jesus probably made some pronouncement about children and God's domain to correspond to his congratulations to the poor, hungry, and sad. Whether the original disciples opposed his openness to children is uncertain; such opposition may reflect resistance in the Christian community in Mark's day.

Disciples and discipleship

3:1–5
MARK 1:16–20

The Fellows agreed by a substantial majority that Jesus had been a disciple of John the Baptist and that some followers of John subsequently became disciples of Jesus. It therefore seems likely that Jesus first met some of his key followers during his connection with the Baptist in the Jordan valley. This fact, together with the stereotypical character of the call stories in Mark 1:16–20, prompted the Fellows to color these accounts gray.

Luke substitutes the anecdote about the miraculous catch of fish (5:1–11) for Mark's twin stories. The Fellows were clear that Luke's account was a Lukan invention. It was therefore designated black.

The twin stories in the Gospel of John (1:35–42, 43–51) were also colored black as fictions, even though the Fellows agreed that Jesus probably recruited his first disciples from among followers of John. Elements in the Johannine version clearly reflect Christian perspectives (for example, John recognizes Jesus as "the lamb of God," and Philip tells Nathanael that "We've found the one Moses wrote about in the Law, and the prophets mention too."). John's version may be correct in indicating that Jesus first recruited disciples from among John's followers while they were all still working in the Jordan valley.

3:8–10
LUKE 8:1–3
This is a Lukan summary; the notice that Mary of Magdala had been freed of seven demons and the mention of the women in v. 14 may be fictions supplied by Luke (the Fellows colored these notices gray).

3:11–12
LUKE 9:57–58
The saying is authentically Jesus; the setting may be contrived.

3:13–14
LUKE 9:59–60
Once again the saying is authentically Jesus, but the setting may be fictitious.

Teaching with authority

4:1–2
MARK 1:21–22
Mark created these verses as a narrative transition. Because they represent typical Christian exaggeration, the Fellows designated them gray. Yet Jesus did appear to teach on his own authority, using parable and witticism, without calling on other authorities. Jesus also appears to have spoken frequently in local synagogues. Aside from the exaggeration, these verses are probably an accurate characterization of Jesus' teaching style.

Demons by the finger of God

5:1–5
MARK 1:35–39

The Fellows decided that it was highly probable that Jesus practiced prayer in seclusion, that he preached in the synagogues of Galilee, and that he drove out what were thought to be demons. Although colored black in *The Acts of Jesus* as a fiction, this story is included here because it depicts typical activities of the historical Jesus. In other words, the story is what may be called a "true fiction."

5:6–11
MARK 1:23–28

This is a standard account of an exorcism: the demon recognizes the exorcist; the exorcist orders the demon to depart with a command; the demon obeys under protest; bystanders verify the cure. The Fellows were dubious that the story as Mark (and Luke 4:33–37) report it is a description of a specific event. They therefore colored it gray, as they did all the other accounts of exorcism. Nevertheless, the Seminar concluded that Jesus did practice exorcism and that this story reflects that practice.

5:17
LUKE 11:20

Matthew's version (12:28) reads: "But if by God's spirit I drive out demons, then for you God's imperial rule has arrived."

5:21–28
MARK 7:24–30

The Fellows were relatively certain that this anecdote contains a kernel of historical truth. Yet they could not agree on precisely which elements were historical and which fictions. They were agreed, however, that Jesus and the woman had an exchange of witticisms in which the woman got the better of Jesus. They concluded that it was unlikely the disciples would have invented such a story for their hero. Since it is impossible to edit out the fictional parts of the anecdote, the entire story was included in *The Gospel of Jesus*.

5:29–31
LUKE 11:24–26   It was usually assumed that exorcised demons did not return to their previous human hosts. Yet this saying suggests that demons, once deprived of a human home, were thought to wander through "waterless places" seeking a new abode. (Demons were thought to inhabit "wet places," such as outhouses and springs and human bodies.) When they are unable to relocate, it was assumed that they would eventually return to their previous habitation, bring additional vile spirits with them, thereby making the second condition of the possessed worse than at first.

Death of John the Baptist

6:1–12
MARK 6:14–29   The story of the beheading of John the Baptist probably reflects historical fact. Details of the story are undoubtedly the product of the storyteller's imagination, but the basic elements may well be accurate. John the Baptist probably did criticize Herod Antipas for his wife-swapping proclivities, and Herodias, Herod's new wife, may have held a grudge against John as a consequence. The role Salome, Herodias' daughter, played in the story is probably fictive, but the beheading of John is not. He was probably executed at Herod's wilderness palace at Machaerus. Other details of the story recorded by Mark are too far-fetched to be treated as historical. Luke omits the account of John's beheading.

Love and forgiveness

7:1
MARK 2:13   This is one of Mark's narrative connectives. In it Mark depicts Jesus as frequenting the Sea of Galilee, where he was often surrounded by crowds. Naturally, the teacher could do nothing other than teach. These typifications the Fellows regarded as essentially accurate.

7:2–4

LUKE 6:27, 32–33

Matthew's version (5:44, 46–47) varies slightly from Luke:

> 44"Love your enemies. 46Tell me, if you love those who love you, why should you be commended for that? Even the toll collectors do as much, don't they? 47And if you greet only your friends, what have you done that is exceptional? Even the pagans do as much, don't they?"

7:20–30

JOHN 8:3–11

The Fellows gave the story of the woman accused of adultery a gray rating. Yet, because it represents Jesus associating with sinners and as an advocate of mercy, the Fellows thought it might reflect the disposition of the historical Jesus. It is what might be called a true fiction. In any case, it is a fragment of a lost gospel that somehow got attached to the Gospel of John in some early manuscripts.

Jesus at the table

8:1–5

MARK 2:15–17

We have omitted certain phrases from the fictive narrative frame.

8:6–7

LUKE 15:1–2

Luke has created this transitional connective; it has no parallels in Mark or Matthew. Yet it appears to be typical of Jesus' public life, as indicated by other anecdotes in the gospels. The Fellows gave it a gray designation but took it to be representative of Jesus' activity and the response to it.

8:8–9

MARK 2:18–19

Mark 2:20–21 are additions of the evangelist or some storyteller before him:

> 20"But the days will come when the groom is taken away from then, and then on that day they will fast.
> 21Nobody sews a piece of unshrunk cloth on an old garment, otherwise the new, unshrunk patch pulls away from the old and creates a worse tear."

The addition indicates how the Christian community restored fasting among its practices without contradicting its memory of the historical Jesus, who did not fast. The addition also indicates how Christian evangelists regarded the new (Christian) as superior to the old (Judaism).

8:10–11
THOM 47:3–4

In this saying, the old is still superior to the new. However, as Christian lore developed, the tendency was to reverse the relationship: the new (Christian) became superior to the old (Judaism). Luke even quotes the common proverb, "Aged wine is just fine" (Luke 5:39b). The Fellows judged the version in Thomas and Luke (5:37–39) to be a pre-Christian version and therefore something the historical Jesus might have said.

Celebration

9:1–5
LUKE 7:31–35

The Fellows were divided in their interpretation of this complex. Some thought that the reference in v. 4 to the "son of Adam" (here translated "this mother's son") precluded the possibility that the complex stemmed from Jesus. Others held that the phrase was Jesus' way of referring to himself in the third person. A divided vote yielded a gray average. Yet all the Fellows agreed that the characterizations fit what we otherwise know of Jesus and John the Baptist.

9:11–12
MATT 13:44

The version in Thomas (109) has developed along different lines. In the Thomas version, the person who discovers the treasure becomes a moneylender—in Thomas (95) a forbidden occupation:

"The Father's imperial rule is like a person who had a treasure hidden in his field but did not know it. 2And when he died he left it to his son. The son did not know about it either. He took over the field and sold it. ³The buyer went plowing, discovered the treasure, and began to lend money at interest to whomever he wished."

9:13–14
THOM 76:1–2

Matthew's alternate version (13:45–46) reads:

⁴⁵Again, Heaven's imperial rule is like some trader looking for beautiful pearls. ⁴⁶When that merchant finds one priceless pearl, he sells everything he owns and buys it."

Sabbath observance

10:5–11
MARK 3:1–5

The Fellows of the Jesus Seminar, in concert with many other scholars, concluded that this story is largely fictive. However, because they think it may contain the kernel of a historical event, they colored it gray. The Fellows believe that Jesus questioned sabbath regulations on at least one occasion (pink), and this story along with Luke 14:1–6 was the basis of that decision. Thus while the story does not depict an actual event, it may well reflect the kind of liberties Jesus took with sabbath restrictions.

Kinship in the kingdom

11:1–3
MARK 3:20–21

Both Matthew and Luke chose to suppress the tradition that Jesus' family thought him demon-possessed—mad. However, the rumor is also reported in the Gospel of John (10:19–21), and it is unlikely that the Christian storytellers would have invented the charge.

11:4
JOHN 10:20

The charge that many people thought Jesus mad is less certain than that his family believed him to be out of his mind—the latter surely would not have been invented by the Christian community. The Fellows colored the statement in the Gospel of John gray. It is included here because it lends credence to the Markan story.

11:5–9
MARK 3:31–35

The Thomas version (99) reads:

"The disciples said to him, `Your brothers and your mother are standing outside.'

"²He said to them, `Those here who do what my Father wants are my brothers and my mother. ³They are the ones who will enter my Father's domain.'"

11:10–11
LUKE 14:25–26

The narrative setting in v. 10 is probably a fiction of the evangelist.

11:12–19
MARK 6:1–6

The narrative connective in v. 12 is a fiction of Mark, yet the incident probably did take place in his hometown.

In parables

12:1–3
MARK 4:1-2

The author of the Gospel of Mark depicts Jesus teaching a crowd from a boat on the Sea of Galilee. These are typifications and are not intended to represent a single event. Mark affixes a collection of parables to this introduction in 4:1–34. We have followed his example, except that the collection of parables employed in *The Gospel of Jesus* is rather different than the one Mark put together.

Public and private piety

13:1
MATT 6:6

The weighted average fell into the gray category, although 58% of the Fellows voted red or pink. The debate centered on whether Jesus had anything to say about prayer.

13:2–4
LUKE 11:2

Jesus' mode of addressing God should be compared with a regulation found in the Manual of Discipline, one of the Dead Sea Scrolls. The Manual contains a charter for the Essene communities, including the one at Qumran. Among the regulations is this (col. 6:27–7:2): "Anyone who speaks aloud the Most Holy Name of God, whether as a curse or simply blurts it out when under duress, or for any other reason, or while he is reading a book or praying, is to be expelled, never to be readmitted to the community." In contrast, Jesus playfully combines an informal, even familiar address ("Abba" which means father), with the admonition to revere the Holy Name, viz. Yahweh, which he apparently never employs. There is a hint of humor in this combination.

Jesus and purity

14:1–5
MARK 7:1–5

The criticism is here directed against Jesus' disciples (v. 2), which suggests that the report may have been assimilated to the situation in Galilee after the death of Jesus, perhaps even after the destruction of the temple in 70 c.e. Nevertheless, it seems likely that Jesus failed to observe all the purity codes and so may have drawn criticism for not washing his hands in the traditional fashion prior to eating. This facet of his behavior comports with his refusal to observe kosher and his willingness to eat with persons considered unclean.

14:6–8
MARK 7:14–16

The saying in v. 8 is probably a cliché that Jesus may or may not have employed. It has been added now and again after sayings, especially those difficult to understand. Because it is probably something many teachers said to their pupils, the Fellows colored it gray.

Signs of God's imperial rule

15:1–3
MARK 8:11–13

It is very probable that people in Jesus' day expected prophets to be able to provide some special omen to demonstrate that they had been authorized by God to say and do what they were saying and doing. Jesus is believed to have refused such requests, as this anecdote indicates.

15:8–10
LUKE 17:20–21

This saying and the preceding one are probably derived from the same original—if there was a single prototype.

Five cures

16:1–2
MATT 8:14–15

Matthew's is a simpler version of the anecdote in Mark (1:29–31).

16:3–5
MARK 1:40–42

The Egerton Gospel version (EgerG 2) is derived from oral tradition, and, because it does not reproduce any of the idiosyncrasies found in Mark, it represents an independent source. It has some interesting variations on the story:

> Just then a leper comes up to him and says, "Teacher, Jesus, in wandering around with lepers and eating with them in the inn, I became a leper myself. ²If you want to, I'll be made clean." ³The master said to him, "Okay—you're clean!" And at once his leprosy vanished from him.

16:6–15
MARK 2:1–9, 12

Although they designated parts of this story gray, the Fellows were relatively certain that Jesus told a lame man to pick up his mat; they were also confident that Jesus healed a lame man.

16:16–19
MARK 5:24–34

As printed here, this story has been edited down to its core, which may well reflect an actual event in the career of the historical Jesus. Either the evangelist or storytellers prior to him elaborated the story by providing fictive details to make it more impressive.

16:20–22
MARK 8:22–24

Jesus probably cured one or more persons of blindness during his career. The kind of blindness he was able to cure was subject to psychosomatic therapy; blindness that had an organic basis would have required magic for a cure and Jesus was probably not a magician. According to the Gospel of John, Peter and Andrew were from Bethsaida, a fishing village on the northern shore of the Sea of Galilee (1:44). Jesus is also reported to have cured Blind Bartimaeus (Mark 10:46–52) and the man born blind (John 9:1–7).

Success, wealth and God's domain

17:1
MARK 10:1
At some point in his public career, Jesus decided to go south to Judea and Jerusalem. His way south may have prompted him to cross the Jordan close to the Sea of Galilee, walk south in Transjordan, and then recross the Jordan at Jericho. By using this route he would have avoided contact with Samaritans who were sometimes hostile to pilgrims on their way to Jerusalem. The geography of Mark is somewhat garbled: he says that Jesus crossed the Jordan into the territory of Judea, which did not extend east of the Jordan. Nevertheless, the general movement of Jesus southward is probably historical. As an itinerant, Jesus undoubtedly taught as he walked along. Locating Jesus' departure for Jerusalem at this point in the story is purely arbitrary both in Mark and in *The Gospel of Jesus*.

17:10–13
THOM 63:1–4
The saying, "Anyone here with two good ears had better listen!" is frequently appended by scribes to difficult aphorisms and to explanations. It is a cliché and is therefore not particularly distinctive. Since it occurs in early Christian texts dozens of times, the Fellows assigned it to the gray category.

Hospitality

18:8–10
LUKE 10:5, 7–8
The peace greeting, "shalom," was a standard greeting on entering someone's house. Because it doesn't tell anything specific about Jesus, the Fellows designated this verse (v. 8) gray.

Sight and light

19:1–10
MARK 10:46–52
According to the sequence of events in Mark, Jesus now recrosses the Jordan at Jericho on his way up to Jerusalem (10:46). He there encounters a blind beggar who addresses him as "Son of David," implying that he was the counter-

part of Solomon who was famous for his miraculous cures. The correlation of trust with cure in v. 7 (Mark 10:52) is a Markan motif that appears elsewhere in his stories of cures. The note that the blind beggar, now with his sight restored, became a follower of Jesus is probably also a Markan touch. The core of the story, which reports the cure of a blind man, may well be historical. It is comparable to the account of the blind man of Bethsaida, 16:20–22, above. In both cases Jesus was performing psychosomatic therapy.

A similar story is found in John 9:1–7, the man born blind:

As he was leaving he saw a man who had been blind from birth. 2His disciples asked him, "Rabbi, was it this man's wrongdoing or his parents' that caused him to be born blind?"

3Jesus responded, "This fellow did nothing wrong, nor did his parents. Rather, he was born blind so God could display his work through him. 4We must carry out the work of the one who sent me while the light lasts. Nighttime is coming and then no one will be able to undertake any work. 5So long as I am in the world I am the light of the world."

6With that he spat on the ground, made mud with his spit and treated the man's eyes with the mud. 7Then Jesus said to him, "Go, rinse off in the pool of Siloam" (the name means "Emissary"). So he went over, rinsed his eyes off, and came back with his sight restored.

It is possible that this story in the Gospel of John and the report of the blind man of Bethsaida (16:20–22) may have evolved from the same basic incident. The cure is effected with spittle in both cases. Or, the Johannine report may have been developed out of the account of Blind Bartimaeus. It is impossible to reconstruct the history of these reports with confidence. Yet it seems likely that the cure of at least one blind person circulated in the oral traditions about Jesus at an early time. The propensity of the evangelists to alter and elaborate reports at will does not breed confidence in the specific details of any of the versions.

In Jerusalem

20:1–2
MARK 11:15, 17

It appears highly likely that Jesus created an incident in the temple area, possibly by objecting to the commercialization of the temple cult (the selling of sacrificial animals and the banking necessary to change money for people so they could pay the temple tax). The temple area was enormous—thirty-five acres in extent—so Jesus could not have cleared the area of hundreds of pilgrims and he could not have prevented merchants from plying their trade. Had he tried to do so, he would have been arrested on the spot. Nevertheless, Jesus probably precipitated some incident in which he criticized the temple cult (as suggested by v. 1, Mark 11:15) and that may have been a factor in his ultimate arrest and execution.

20:3–4
THOM 100:1–3

The version in the Gospel of Mark (12:13–17) reads:

¹³And they send some of the Pharisees and the Herodians to him to trap him with a riddle. ¹⁴They come and say to him, "Teacher, we know that you are honest and impartial, because you pay no attention to appearances, but instead you teach God's way forthrightly. Is it permissible to pay the poll tax to the Roman emperor or not? Should we pay or should we not pay?"

But he saw through their trap, and said to them, "Why do you provoke me like this? Let me have a look at a coin."

¹⁶They handed him a silver coin, and he says to them, "Whose picture is this? Whose name is on it?"

They replied, "The emperor's."

¹⁷Jesus said to them: "Pay the emperor what belongs to the emperor, and God what belongs to God!" And they were dumbfounded at him.

The Thomas version preserves the core of the original story, which Mark has elaborated into a full-blown narrative segment. In Mark, v. 13 is part of the evangelist's conspiracy theory: Jesus was the victim of a conspiracy against him. The anecdote that develops the riddle and Jesus' clever reply is told in the style of the pronouncement stories so common in hellenistic lore. However, the aphorism reported in both Thomas and Mark probably goes back to Jesus.

20:5–11
JOHN 5:2–3, 5–9

The Fellows colored this story gray because the fourth evangelist has taken an older healing story and revised it to suit the new context he has devised for it. The Johannine story may have been derived ultimately from the same tale that Mark reports in 2:1–12 (16:6–15 above).

The passion

21:2
JOHN 18:1–2

The statements in this and the preceding verse were colored gray by the Fellows. However, a narrative statement to the effect that those who knew Jesus turned him in by taking the temple authorities to the place drew a pink vote. In other words, the Fellows agreed by a slim majority that some of Jesus' followers betrayed the place where the authorities might find him. Jesus himself did not require identification.

Pillars and Pioneers

epil 1–3
PSMARK 16:9–11

This text is derived from PsMark 16:9–11, which the Seminar colored black. It is used here to express the judgment of the Fellows that Mary of Magdala was the first to come to the resurrection faith. That conviction is based in part on the account in John 20:1–2, 11–18, which, unfortunately, is linked to the empty tomb story. When the Fellows colored the Johannine version of the appearance to Mary gray, they did so because they could not find Mary's claim expressed elsewhere without ties to the empty tomb. Further, they agreed on two points: Mary was the first to have a vision of the risen Jesus; those to whom Mary reported her experience did not at first believe her. The words of Pseudo-Mark seemed to be the best vehicle to express these two judgments. Of course, the unedited text of Pseudo-Mark does connect Mary's vision with the Easter Sunday morning at the tomb, but in this case it was easily possible to eliminate that connection. On the other hand, the editor saw no way to disentangle the Johannine version of Mary's encounter with the risen Jesus from the setting at the tomb.

THE JESUS SEMINAR IS COMPOSED of gospel scholars dedicated to the advancement of the quest of the historical Jesus. The members of the Seminar, called Fellows, are professional biblical scholars, most of whom teach in colleges, universities, or theological seminaries. The Seminar is not sponsored, supervised, endorsed, or funded by any academic or religious organization. Anyone with the appropriate academic credentials can become a Fellow, regardless of religious commitments or point of view. About two hundred scholars have participated in the deliberations since its inception. Seventy-five have signed each of the two major reports. The Seminar has met twice a year since 1985.

The Fellows who formed the Jesus Seminar agreed to do certain things at the outset. We agreed to form an agenda and come to decision on the basis of the best knowledge we had at the time and in light of our best judgments. We adopted collaboration as our group process in order to expand the base of decision-making and we agreed to make our work cumulative, which meant that we had to identify or form a consensus and then build on that consensus. We welcomed the broadest spectrum of opinion we could enlist in order to make our membership genuinely ecumenical. We eventually learned to stop posturing and pretending; we developed a penchant for honesty and candor. And most important of all, we agreed to conduct our deliberations in public—in the presence of our Associate members—and to report the results to a broad, literate audience in simple, non-technical prose.

Agenda

We set out to inventory the data—all the data—that has survived in ancient documents produced before about 325 c.e. We did not limit ourselves to the four New Testament gospels; we avoided canonical bias by including all twenty-one (now twenty-two) gospels. We then classified the data by sorting into types of sayings and types of stories. The big job was to assess the data, item by item, for historical information. During the

107

years we have worked together, the Seminar has sorted through about 1500 versions of approximately five hundred sayings ascribed to Jesus, and has identified those words that, in the judgment of the Fellows of the Seminar, were most probably spoken by him. We wound up with a compendium of about ninety authentic sayings and parables.

When we had completed that task, we turned to the 387 reports of 176 events and deeds and carried out a similar evaluation. Twenty-nine of 176 events were deemed to contain historical information.

The result was the creation of a twin database: The first was published as *The Five Gospels* (1993), the second as *The Acts of Jesus*, which appeared in 1998.

It was not until we had finished the first two phases of our work that we permitted ourselves to interpret that database. Our interpretations took the form of profiles of Jesus prepared by individual Fellows. Profiles of Jesus comprise the third phase of the Seminar, a phase that came to an end in 1999.

Voting

After careful study and debate, the Fellows of the Seminar vote to express our judgments on historical questions. Voting is a traditional method among biblical scholars to determine whether or not there is a consensus and if so, what its magnitude may be. Voting is done by colored beads, the meaning of which is formulated below.

Sayings

    Red: Jesus undoubtedly said this or something very like it.

    Pink: Jesus probably said something like this.

    Gray: Jesus did not say this, but the ideas contained in it are close to his own.

    Black: Jesus did not say this; it represents the perspective or content of a later or different tradition.

Deeds

Red: The historical reliability of this information is virtually certain. It is supported by a preponderance of evidence.

Pink: This information is probably reliable. It fits well with other evidence that is verifiable.

Gray: This information is possible but unreliable. It lacks supporting evidence.

Black: This information is improbable. It does not fit verifiable evidence; it is largely or entirely fictive.

The results are an average of all the votes cast. Every vote helps determine the final color; every vote counts because the average is a weighted average.

Reporting

In *The Five Gospels* and *The Acts of Jesus*, we color-coded the results of our deliberations and endeavored to give a brief account of how we reached our conclusions. Our intention in creating a color-coded report was to make its contents immediately evident to the general reader without the necessity of reading hundreds of pages of commentary. In addition, it took as its model the red-letter editions of the New Testament widely known among readers of the Bible. *The Five Gospels* was on the religion best-seller list for nine months.

Sayings Gospels

1. Sayings Gospel Q
2. Gospel of Thomas
3. Gospel Oxyrhynchus 1224
4. Secret Book of James
5. Dialogue of the Savior
6. Gospel of Mary

Narrative Gospels

7. Gospel of Mark
8. Gospel of Matthew
9. Gospel of Luke
10. Signs Gospel
11. Gospel of John
12. Gospel of Peter
13. Secret Mark
14. Egerton Gospel
15. Gospel Oxyrhynchus 840
16. First Stone Gospel
17. Gospel of the Hebrews
18. Gospel of the Nazoreans
19. Gospel of the Ebionites
20. Gospel of the Savior

Infancy Gospels

21. Infancy Gospel of Thomas
22. Infancy Gospel of James

The New Testament Gospels

There are four New Testament gospels, as everyone knows. Their order in conventional New Testaments is: Matthew, Mark, Luke, John. Since Mark is the earliest of the four and the probable basis of both Matthew and Luke, in the Scholars Version we have moved Mark to the first position. These gospels, which are narrative gospels (not just collections of Jesus' sayings), provide us with the bulk of basic information we have about Jesus.

Gospel of Mark

An anonymous author composed the Gospel of Mark shortly after the destruction of the Jerusalem temple in 70 C.E. Mark may be responsible for forming the first chronological outline of the life of Jesus. He may also be responsible for the first connected account of Jesus' trial and crucifixion, usually referred to as the passion story. The author reflects the early Christian view that God was about to bring history to an end in an apocalyptic conflagration.

The Gospel of Mark was attributed to John Mark, a companion of Paul and perhaps an associate of Peter. This attribution, like many others in the ancient world, is the product of pious speculation.

Mark's gospel became the basis for the gospels of Matthew and Luke.

Gospel of Matthew

An anonymous author compiled the Gospel of Matthew sometime after the fall of Jerusalem and before the Council of Jamnia in 90 C.E. This is the period in which the Christian community, probably in Syria, was seeking its own identify over against emerging Rabbinic Judaism. The new form of Judaism was attempting to recover from the loss of its center of worship, the temple. Matthew is usually dated to about 85 C.E.

Matthew was composed in Greek. The author made use of both the Sayings Gospel Q and the Gospel of Mark. It is incor-

111

rect to say that Matthew was composed in Hebrew by one of the original disciples of Jesus.

Gospel of Luke

Luke-Acts, a two-volume work by a single author, depicts the emergence of Christianity on the world stage. It was composed around 90 C.E., slightly later than Matthew. Whereas Matthew was concerned with the relation between the Christian movement and Judaism, Luke is preoccupied with developments in the gentile world.

The tradition that Luke the physician and companion of Paul was the author goes back to the second century. However, it is highly improbable that Luke was a physician and he almost certainly was not a companion of Paul. As in the case of the other gospels, the author is unknown.

Gospel of John

The Gospel of John was allegedly written by John, son of Zebedee, one of an inner group of Jesus' companions. According to legend, John lived to a ripe old age in Ephesus where he composed the gospel, three letters, and possibly the book of Revelation. This legend is fictive.

The Gospel of John was probably composed toward the close of the first century C.E., which makes it a close contemporary of Matthew and Luke. It exhibits evidence of having gone through several editions. Many scholars therefore conclude that John is the product of a "school," which may indeed have been formed by the John of the legend.

Its place of origin is unknown. It was clearly created in a hellenistic city of some magnitude with a strong Jewish community. A city in Asia Minor or Syria, or possibly Alexandria in Egypt, would do.

It is uncertain whether John knew the synoptic gospels—Mark, Matthew, Luke—so-called because they take a common view of the life of Jesus, based as they all are on Mark. The Johannine school may have made use of a "signs" source, which consisted of a series of miraculous deeds presumably performed by Jesus.

In addition to the four New Testament gospels, there were at least eighteen other gospels, sixteen of which have survived from antiquity, either in whole or in part. The other two are hypothetical reconstructions.

Sayings Gospels

Sayings Gospel Q

In the view of a great many scholars, Matthew and Luke once knew and used a written collection of the sayings of Jesus in composing their own gospels. If this hypothesis is correct, that source may well have been among the very first gospels reduced to writing. Although it did not survive as a separate document, this collection of Jesus' sayings became an important part of Matthew and Luke. That lost gospel has been dubbed Q from a German word meaning "source" (*Quelle*); it is now usually referred to as the Sayings Gospel Q. A reconstructed Q may be found in *The Complete Gospels.*

Gospel of Thomas

The Gospel of Thomas is also a sayings gospel. It contains 114 sayings ascribed to Jesus. It lacks narrative connectives; it does not have a passion story, or appearance stories, or birth and childhood stories. The Coptic text of Thomas was discovered at Nag Hammadi, a place in upper Egypt, in 1945. Three Greek fragments of Thomas had been discovered earlier, but scholars were unable to identify them as fragments of Thomas until the Coptic text was unearthed. There is about a 40% overlap between Q and Thomas.

Gospel Oxyrhynchus 1224

Two tiny fragments of a gospel whose name is unknown were discovered in 1903 at Oxyrhynchus in Egypt. It contains some very fragmentary sayings of Jesus and has thus been classified as a sayings gospel.

Secret Book of James & Dialogue of the Savior

Two other gospels from Nag Hammadi, Secret James and the Dialogue of the Savior, also provide some data about Jesus, but they have not contributed significantly to the advance of knowledge.

Gospel of Mary

The Gospel of Mary was discovered among papyrus fragments in the Berlin Museum. There are also some scraps of a Greek version of Mary, just as there are Greek scraps of the Gospel of Thomas. Unfortunately, the center portion of Mary is missing. It is still unclear what we will learn from the study of the Gospel of Mary, although Mary is primarily a sayings rather than a narrative gospel.

Other Narrative Gospels

The Signs Gospel

Some scholars believe that a collection of signs that Jesus performed was the precursor of the Gospel of John. Attempts have been made to reconstruct it from the text of John. The Signs Gospel appears to have some stories in common with a similar sequence of miracles in the Gospel of Mark.

The Gospel of Peter

The Gospel of Peter is a fragmentary report of the passion and resurrection of Jesus. Some scholars believe Peter preserves the earliest narrative of the events surrounding the arrest, trial, and crucifixion of Jesus. It has turned out to be part of the fundamental debate about the value of our sources.

Secret Mark

Two brief fragments from an early version of the Gospel of Mark were discovered in 1958 and published in 1973. It is called Secret Mark because this version was believed to be intended for only those who had reached a higher stage of initiation. The rest of Secret Mark has been lost, at least for the present. The two fragments confirm once again that the gospels went through more than one edition in their earlier stages.

Egerton Gospel

The Egerton Gospel is known from a single cluster of fragments that can be dated to the middle of the second century. It preserves a few anecdotes about Jesus that may contain some independent testimony. Egerton is the name of the donor who gave the money to purchase the fragments. Like most other manuscripts of the gospels, Egerton comes from Egypt.

Gospel Oxyrhynchus 840

This gospel is a tiny vellum fragment of a narrative gospel written in a tiny script. It was probably used as an amulet by some Christian folk. Most of the remaining text is devoted to a dispute over purity in the temple precincts. The handwriting suggests that the copy was made in the fourth century c.e., although the composition of this gospel probably took place much earlier.

First Stone Gospel

The story of the woman accused of adultery and brought to Jesus appears in manuscripts of the Gospels of John and Luke. It is what scholars call a floating segment or orphan text. It probably comes from another earlier narrative gospel, the balance of which was lost. The first stone segment survived by being copied into John or Luke.

The Jewish-Christian Gospels

According to some of the scholars of the early church—called Church Fathers—there were three Jewish-Christian gospels: Ebionites, Hebrews, and Nazoreans, by name. The Fathers preserve a few scattered quotations from these gospels. They must be added to our list of sources.

The Gospel of the Savior

Recently, fragments of the Gospel of the Savior were discovered in the Berlin Egyptian Museum by Charles Hedrick and Paul Mirecki. The Gospel of the Savior survives only in Coptic, like the Nag Hammadi Codices. It consists of a dialogue between the savior and the apostles. The author seems to have been acquainted with both the Matthean and the Johannine traditions. The fragments are to be dated from the fourth to the seventh centuries c.e. They will probably contribute very little new information to the quest for the historical Jesus.

The Infancy Gospels

There are also two infancy gospels, Infancy James and Infancy Thomas (not to be confused with the Gospel of Thomas) that betray how extensively the myths and legends about the young Jesus and his young mother developed in the second and third centuries. Neither of these gospels is especially helpful in reconstructing the history of Jesus. That inventory brings to twenty-two the number of gospels from which data may be extracted for reconstructing a profile of the historical Jesus.

Other Sources

Eusebius (?260–?340) was bishop of Caesarea and confidant of the Emperor Constantine at the Council of Nicea (325 C.E.). His most important work is his *Ecclesiastical History*, which is the principal source for our knowledge of the history of Christianity from the apostolic age to his own day.

Hegesippus was a Jewish-Christian church historian of the 2nd century C.E. (precise dates unknown), who wrote five *Books of Memoirs* in opposition to the Gnostics. His works have disappeared, although they are quoted extensively by Eusebius in his *Ecclesiastical History*.

Josephus, Flavius (?37–?100) was a Jewish historian who wrote two major histories: *The Jewish War*, which is an account of events leading up to and including the Jewish war with the Romans, 66–73 C.E. The second work is called *The Antiquities of the Jews* in twenty books (scrolls), which sketches the history of the Jews from the creation to the beginning of the Jewish war.

Stage 1: 50–70 C.E.

Sayings Gospel Q
First edition of Thomas
Gospel Oxyrhynchus 1224
Signs Gospel

Stage 2: 70–80

Gospel of Mark
Egerton Gospel

Stage 3: 80–90

Gospel of Matthew
Gospel of Luke

Stage 4: 90–100

Gospel of John

Stage 5: 100–150

Gospel of Peter
Gospel of Mary
Secret Mark
Infancy Gospel of James
Infancy Gospel of Thomas
Secret James
The Amulet Gospel (Gospel Oxyrhynchus 840)
Dialogue of the Savior

Stage 6: 150 and beyond

Gospel of the Ebionites
Gospel of the Hebrews
Gospel of the Nazoreans
Gospel of the Savior

The Complete Gospels, ed. Robert J. Miller. 3rd ed.
Polebridge Press, 1994.

This volume is indispensable for those interested in the quest. It has modern translations of twenty-one gospels. The twenty-second will be added to a new edition in the near future.

The primary reports of the Jesus Seminar containing color-coded evaluations of all the words and deeds ascribed to Jesus are:

The Five Gospels: The Search for the Authentic Words of Jesus, Robert W. Funk, Roy W. Hoover, and the Jesus Seminar. HarperSanFrancisco/Polebridge Press, 1993.

In *The Five Gospels,* the Jesus Seminar examined approximately 1,500 version of five hundred sayings, parables, and dialogues attributed to Jesus. The results of the Seminar's deliberations are reported by colored-coding the texts of all five gospels (Mark, Matthew, Luke, John and Thomas).

The Acts of Jesus: The Search for the Authentic Deeds of Jesus, Robert W. Funk and The Jesus Seminar. HarperSanFrancisco/Polebridge Press, 1998.

In *The Acts of Jesus,* the Fellows reviewed 387 reports of 176 events reported in all the gospels. They again reported the results of their debates by color-coding all 387 anecdotes.

The Parables of Jesus: Red Letter Edition, Robert W. Funk, Brandon B. Scott, and James R. Butts. Polebridge Press, 1988.

The Parables of Jesus is a color-coded report on sixty versions of thirty-three parables attributed to Jesus in a handy 108-page booklet. This was the first public report issued by the Seminar.

John the Baptist and Jesus: A Report of the Jesus Seminar,
W. Barnes Tatum. Polebridge Press, 1993.

W. Barnes Tatum has provided a concise account of the quest of the historical John the Baptist in this report. The author has sketched the color-coded decisions of the Jesus Seminar along with a lucid analysis of how the Seminar reached its conclusions.

The Jesus Seminar is a project of the Westar Institute, a membership-supported, nonprofit research and educational organization for the promotion of biblical and religious literacy.

Associate membership in Westar Institute is open to all interested individuals. For more information contact:

Westar Institute
P. O. Box 6144
Santa Rosa, CA 95406
(707) 523-1323
Fax (707) 523-1350
www.westarinstitute.org

120